CONFIDENCE POC

CONFIDENCE POCKETBOOK

LITTLE EXERCISES FOR A SELF-ASSURED LIFE

Gill Hasson

CAPSTONE
A Wiley Brand

This edition first published 2017.
© 2017 Gill Hasson

Registered office
John Wiley & Sons Ltd, The Atrium, Southern Gate, Chichester, West Sussex, PO19 8SQ, United Kingdom

For details of our global editorial offices, for customer services and for information about how to apply for permission to reuse the copyright material in this book please see our website at www.wiley.com.

Wiley publishes in a variety of print and electronic formats and by print-on-demand. Some material included with standard print versions of this book may not be included in e-books or in print-on-demand. If this book refers to media such as a CD or DVD that is not included in the version you purchased, you may download this material at http://booksupport.wiley.com. For more information about Wiley products, visit www.wiley.com.

Designations used by companies to distinguish their products are often claimed as trademarks. All brand names and product names used in this book are trade names, service marks, trademarks or registered trademarks of their respective owners. The publisher is not associated with any product or vendor mentioned in this book.

Limit of Liability/Disclaimer of Warranty: While the publisher and author have used their best efforts in preparing this book, they make no representations or warranties with respect to the accuracy or completeness of the contents of this book and specifically disclaim any implied warranties of merchantability or fitness for a particular purpose. It is sold on the understanding that the publisher is not engaged in rendering professional services and neither the publisher nor the author shall be liable for damages arising herefrom. If professional advice or other expert assistance is required, the services of a competent professional should be sought.

Library of Congress Cataloging-in-Publication Data

Names: Hasson, Gill, author.
Title: Confidence pocketbook : little exercises for a self-assured life /
  Gill Hasson.
Description: Chichester, West Sussex, United Kingdom : Wiley, [2017] |
  Identifiers: LCCN 2017011373 (print) | ISBN 9780857087331 (pbk.)
Subjects: LCSH: Self-confidence. | Confidence.
Classification: LCC BF575.S39 H3975 2017 (print) |
  DDC 158.1—dc23
LC record available at https://lccn.loc.gov/2017011373

A catalogue record for this book is available from the British Library.

ISBN 978-0-857-08733-1 (pbk)
ISBN 978-0-857-08734-8 (ebk)
ISBN 978-0-857-08731-7 (ebk)

Cover Design and Illustration: Wiley

Set in 10/12.5pt Rotis Sans Serif Std by Aptara Inc., New Delhi, India

Printed in Great Britain by TJ International Ltd, Padstow, Cornwall, UK

CONTENTS

INTRODUCTION

It is never too late to be what you might have been. —George Eliot

Do you feel that life would improve for you if you had more confidence and self-esteem?

When you're confident and have good self-esteem, you believe in yourself; your decisions, your actions and your abilities. You face life with optimism; you believe that you can cope with challenges and difficulties and that events are likely to turn out well. You value yourself and feel good about yourself. You feel at ease around other people; able to join in, speak up and speak out.

It's a positive dynamic: learn to be more confident in one situation and you'll find it boosts your confidence and self-esteem in other situations; at work, in public, with family and friends and in social situations.

Confidence is life's enabler; life really does improve as your self-confidence and self-esteem grow. So, clearly, confidence is something that's worth pursuing. But how do you begin to improve your confidence? The *Confidence Pocketbook* can help!

There are three parts to the *Confidence Pocketbook*:

- Part 1: The Foundation Stones of Confidence
- Part 2: Personal Confidence
- Part 3: Social Confidence

Self-confidence and self-esteem are built from a sound base of foundation stones. Part 1 of this book explains what those foundation stones are and how you can establish them. The foundation stones involve principles – fundamental truths – which apply in a wide range of situations, both personal and social.

Part 2 – Personal Confidence – addresses specific aspects of your life where you may want to feel more confident and better about yourself and your abilities. Whether you want the confidence to take risks and make mistakes, to travel or return to learn – whatever the issue – simply pick out the ideas, tips and techniques that appeal to you and give them a try.

Part 3 of this book – Social Confidence – addresses a range of issues related to interacting with other people; colleagues, friends, family etc. Whether you want the confidence to speak up or speak out, be treated with respect or make new friends, simply pick out the ideas, tips and techniques that appeal to you and give them a try.

Confidence and self-esteem aren't fixed, they increase and decrease according to the ups and downs you experience in life. Although the way other people treat you and behave towards you has an effect on your confidence, other people can't force you to be confident and feel good about yourself. You have to take responsibility and be prepared to work at developing and maintaining your confidence and self-esteem.

The *Confidence Pocketbook* has over 100 simple confidence tips, techniques, ideas and suggestions for a wide range of situations where you're likely to want to be more confident and capable. The more often you use them, the more you'll develop your confidence and self-esteem.

Keep this book in your bag or your pocket whenever and wherever you need to feel more confident. You'll find that the tips, techniques, ideas and suggestions in this book really can help you act with confidence and feel good about yourself.

It's not about becoming a different person; it's about becoming more of the real you!

PART 1
THE FOUNDATION STONES OF CONFIDENCE

UNDERSTANDING CONFIDENCE

Success comes in cans, not can'ts. —Author unknown

Confidence is a belief that something can and will happen. You may be confident that your team will win. You could be confident the train will arrive on time. Whether the team does actually win or the train does arrive on time is another matter!

Self-confidence is believing that *you* can do things.

Self-confidence is not about what you can or can't do. It's what you think and *believe* you can or can't do. You might believe that you can sky-dive or pass an exam. Whether, when the time comes, you *can* jump out of the plane or pass the exam is also another matter!

When you're feeling confident, you have a positive attitude towards yourself and your abilities and you believe that events and experiences are likely to turn out well. But when you're not feeling confident, you're likely to believe that things will turn out badly. And because you *believe* things won't turn out well, you often feel that there's no point in even trying.

Furthermore, you only see or even look for evidence that confirms that you can't do something while avoiding or ignoring evidence that, actually, you *could* do something. So if you weren't feeling confident about passing your driving test, you'd focus on the weaker aspects of your driving abilities – reverse parking or three-point turns – as evidence that you weren't going to do well.

And, when setbacks do occur, if you lack confidence you're likely to feel discouraged and give up. Whereas if you're feeling confident, you're able to work at overcoming the difficulties, *believing* that things can get better.

In Practice

Believe in yourself! Have faith in your abilities! Without a humble but reasonable confidence in your own powers you cannot be successful or happy. —Norman Vincent Peale

Be more aware of how you think and what you do. When you're lacking confidence in a particular situation, what are you thinking? Do you think things like, 'I can't do it' and 'This is going to be so difficult'? Do you tell yourself, 'It's not going to turn out well – it's going to go wrong'? Do you avoid taking part in or back out of events and situations because you think you're going to feel awkward or fail?

What about when you *are* feeling confident? What thoughts pass through your head? Do you think things like, 'I can do this', 'I'm looking forward to this' or 'Things will work out fine'? Do you tell yourself 'If things don't work out, I'll be able to deal with it'? Maybe, when you're feeling confident you don't even give it any thought – you just get on with doing it.

Identify the evidence. Think of something you would you like to do but don't have the confidence. For example, you might want to learn a new skill, start your own business or go to a social event. Don't believe you can do it? How do you *know* you can't do it? Write down the evidence – the reasons why you think you can't do it. Now write down the evidence – the reasons – that maybe you *could* do it. Which would be more helpful for you to believe – the evidence you could do it, or the evidence that you couldn't do it?

Remember: confidence is not what you can or can't do, it's what you *think* and *believe* you can or can't do.

UNDERSTANDING SELF-ESTEEM

Low self-esteem is like driving through life with your hand-brake on. —Maxwell Maltz

Just as your self-confidence is affected by what you believe about yourself, so is your self-esteem. Confidence rests on what you believe about your *abilities*. Self-esteem rests on what you believe about your *worth* and *value* as a person.

Confidence and self-esteem influence each other. If, in a variety of situations, you don't have confidence – if you don't believe you are capable of doing something – you may also feel bad about yourself; about your perceived inability to do something. You'll have low self-esteem. When your self-esteem is low, you see yourself in a negative and critical light; you see or even look for evidence that confirms that you're not a worthy person while ignoring evidence that you have worth and value. You'll also feel less able to take on the challenges life throws at you, and that just undermines your self-esteem further and you feel bad again. It's a negative dynamic.

On the other hand, building your confidence helps you feel good about yourself. And if you feel good about yourself, you feel more confident about your abilities and life in general. It's a positive dynamic; a win-win situation.

Are you born with self-esteem? Not exactly. You're born with the ability to think and therefore to judge your worth and value; to feel good, bad or somewhere in between about yourself. As you live your life, what happens to you – your experiences, what you do and don't do, and how other people treat you and behave towards you – will influence your self-esteem, for better or worse.

In Practice

You are what you think you are. And what you think, you are.
—Author unknown

The judgements and opinions you have of yourself reflect your levels of self-esteem. Read the statements below. Tick each one you think is *true* about the way you think.

☐ I think I'm as good and likeable as other people.
☐ If I do well at something I feel pleased with myself.
☐ If someone criticises me I deal with it and then move on. I don't let it knock me back too much.
☐ I can say no to others' needs and demands – especially if they're unreasonable.
☐ I think most people I know like me and think I'm a good person.
☐ I don't let others treat me unfairly.
☐ I feel that my opinions and needs matter as much as anyone else's.
☐ If I make a mistake I don't think I'm completely hopeless.
☐ I don't avoid taking part in things because I feel I'm not good enough.
☐ I think I have several good qualities.
☐ I think I am as deserving of respect and happiness as anyone else.
☐ I have achieved things that I feel proud of.
☐ I don't constantly need others' approval.

The fewer statements you ticked, the more likely it is that you have low self-esteem. The good news is that you can develop new, positive ways of seeing yourself and your abilities!

AVOIDING THE
COMPARISON TRAP

Comparison is the thief of joy. —Theodore Roosevelt

Confidence and self-esteem are concerned with what we believe about our abilities and our self-worth.

But how can we judge our worth and abilities? Using what standards and criteria? By comparing our abilities and worth with those of other people.

The problem is, there's always someone you know, meet, see, listen to or read about in magazines, newspapers and on Facebook, who you could see as being 'better': more successful, better looking, more capable or who has more and has done more than you.

You can always find ways that you don't match up. Of course, it's natural to want to know where you fit into the scheme of things. But measuring your worth and your abilities against other people and concluding you don't match up can only lead to feeling inferior, disappointed and even ashamed.

How often, though, do you compare yourself with someone less fortunate than you and consider yourself blessed? Too often, we compare ourselves with someone who we think is 'better' or has more; better skills, abilities or personal qualities and better or more resources and possessions. We compare what we think is the worst of ourselves to the best we presume about others.

You may even look for further evidence to support and confirm what you've decided is true; the negative ways in which you don't match up, what you don't have, can't do or will never be. But these sorts of negative comparisons only create resentment and feelings of unfairness and deprivation.

In Practice

There is nothing noble about being superior to some other man. The true nobility is in being superior to your previous self. —Hindu proverb

Break free of the negative comparison habit. Ask yourself, 'How does comparing myself or my situation to others make me feel?' If comparisons leave you feeling resentful, discouraged and feeling bad about yourself, then clearly it's not helpful to think like this.

Focus on you. Comparing yourself to someone else puts the focus on the wrong person. Your skills, abilities, contributions and value are entirely unique to you. They can never be fairly compared to anyone else. Your time and effort could be better spent thinking positively about yourself. Compare yourself to yourself. Focus on what you have done and are doing rather than what everyone else has done and is doing. Reflect on what you've experienced, achieved and/or overcome. See how far you have come compared to last week, last year, two years ago, five years ago. And if you've suffered a setback, focus on how you can move forward and gain ground again.

Instead of comparing yourself with others, be inspired by others. Rather than compare yourself with other people who are 'better' or have more than you, see others as role models to learn from and inspire you. When you allow yourself to feel inspired by others, you can feel motivated to achieve and do well according to your own abilities, skills and resources.

Compare less. Appreciate more. Being more aware of what you do have rather than what, compared to others, you don't have, is a far more positive direction to take. Identify the good fortune, privileges and qualities you have and build on them.

BEING WITH POSITIVE PEOPLE

Be who you are and say what you feel, because those who mind don't matter and those who matter don't mind. —Dr Seuss

Confidence and self-esteem come not just from what *you* believe about yourself and your abilities but also what other people – family, friends, colleagues etc. – think and believe about you and how they behave towards you and respond to you.

If you believe something about yourself – it could be positive or negative – and other people believe that about you too, then together you make it a reality. In a variety of situations, being positively noticed, encouraged or praised by others can help you build a positive view of yourself. However, not being valued by others and receiving negative responses from other people can make it more likely that you will lack confidence and have low self-esteem.

Throughout your life you come across all kinds of people, different in many ways. But when it comes to how they impact on your self-esteem and confidence, other people can fall into one of two camps: they are either 'drains' or 'radiators.' People who are radiators emanate warmth and positivity, while drains can leave you feeling ... drained. Their negativity can drain your self-esteem and confidence.

So, who you spend most of your time with can make a difference to your self-esteem and confidence. If you have low self-esteem, there might be people who, deliberately or not, encourage negative beliefs and opinions that you may hold about yourself. You need radiators in your life! Positive people are likely to respond to you in positive ways and so help you think positively about yourself and your abilities.

In Practice

Surround yourself with people who make you happy. People who make you laugh, who help you when you're in need. People who genuinely care. They are the ones worth keeping in your life. Everyone else is just passing through. —Karl Marx

Identify the positive people in your life. Which people come to mind from the examples below?

- ☐ Someone I can talk to if I am worried.
- ☐ Someone I can be myself with.
- ☐ Someone who listens to me.
- ☐ Someone who encourages me.
- ☐ Someone who I have fun with.
- ☐ Someone who shares the same interests or hobbies as me.
- ☐ Someone who introduces me to new ideas and interests.
- ☐ Someone who is kind, compassionate and caring.

You may have a different person or a number of people for each situation, or the same one or two people might fit a number of situations. Think widely; the positive people on your list do not just have to be friends or family; they could be colleagues, neighbours or professionals. The person you can talk to if you're worried, for example, could be your GP, a counsellor, someone at a support group or at the end of a helpline. Maybe the person who introduces you to new worlds, ideas and interests is a tutor on a course or an author of interesting books. Perhaps there's a comedian on radio or TV who makes you laugh.

It is not always possible or practical to completely avoid negative people. What you can do, however, is increase the amount of time you spend with 'radiators', the positive people on your list.

DOING THINGS YOU ENJOY

I don't believe people are looking for the meaning of life as much as they are looking for the experience of being alive. —Joseph Campbell

What makes you feel alive? What do you enjoy doing? Swimming, painting or yoga? Maybe you enjoy cooking? Singing? Hiking? Playing guitar? Running? Playing or watching football?

Whenever you're engaged in an activity or interest that you enjoy doing, you are in what is known as a state of 'flow'. Flow refers to time spent doing something that keeps you focused and engaged. You become so absorbed in what you're doing that time just *flows*.

Whatever the activity is, although it might provide a challenge, you know you can do it. You don't feel self-conscious or worry that you can't do it. In other words, you're confident about what you're doing and you enjoy doing it. It stands to reason that the more often you do things you enjoy and can do well, the more you are tapping into and strengthening your confidence and self-esteem.

Often, activities where you experience 'flow' are creative – things like painting, playing music, cooking, sewing, writing and doing arts and crafts. Other activities may be physical: for example, gardening, hiking, horse riding, yoga or tennis. It might be something you do on your own – reading, painting, gardening – or with other people – team sports, board and computer games, singing in a choir, hiking. It might be something you do for half an hour or something you do for a few hours at a time.

We can all experience more enjoyment in our lives; more 'flow'. We just need to consciously choose to create it.

In Practice

It is not how much we have, but how much we enjoy that makes happiness. —Charles Spurgeon

Do more of what you enjoy. When you need a confidence boost, take a step back and return to what you know you do well and enjoy. Are there activities in your life that bring you a sense of satisfaction and make you feel good about yourself and your abilities? Think of the things that you enjoy doing: leisure activities, hobbies, sports, interests. Identify which ones you can do for short periods of time and others which you can do for a few hours. Find ways to do them more often.

Need more enjoyable activities in your life? Here are some ideas.

- Sports activities: tennis, table tennis, football, volleyball, hockey, running, yoga, pilates, swimming or hiking. Or how about rock climbing?
- Sing and dance to music or join a dance class: Lindy Hop, tap, ballet or line dancing. Learn to tango or dance a Rumba. Join a choir – a rock choir, chamber choir or gospel choir. Or simply sing and dance along to your favourite tunes in the kitchen. Learn to play an instrument – guitar, piano, harmonica, trombone – the choice is endless.
- Take up a creative interest: gardening, painting, calligraphy, photography, embroidery, bird watching, juggling, fishing or stamp collecting.
- Play card and board games, computer games, jigsaws, crosswords or sudoku. As with sports activities, singing, dancing and creative activities, you don't need to be amazing, just competent enough to take part and enjoy doing so.

HAVING GOALS TO AIM FOR

The trouble with not having a goal is that you can spend your life running up and down the field and never score. —Bill Copeland

Is there something you want to feel more confident about doing? Good. Because in order to build your confidence you need something specific to direct your efforts towards. You need a goal. It could be a short-term goal; something you want to achieve today, in the next few days or weeks. Or it could be a longer-term goal; something you want to be able to do in the next few months.

Maybe you want the confidence to ask someone to do something for you – your doctor to refer you to a consultant for a health problem you have or your manager to give you a pay rise. Perhaps you want the confidence to sign up to a class or join a club; to take up running or join a sports club, a choir or a theatre company.

Maybe you'd like to work freelance, run your own business, work abroad, or return to study. Maybe you'd like to leave a job, a university course or a relationship. Perhaps you want to travel: drive to Paris, visit Athens or explore Berlin, Costa Rica or Cuba?

Once you've identified something specific you want confidence for, you've identified a goal; something to focus your efforts and work towards.

Wanting to be more confident is meaningless until you attach it to something specific. Setting goals and working to achieve them is an important part of developing your overall confidence and self-esteem. Goals give you something specific to work towards. As you achieve each goal, you create the momentum that helps you continue to build your confidence in a range of other situations.

In Practice

What you get by achieving your goals is not as important as what you become by achieving your goals. —Zig Ziglar

Commit yourself. Think of a specific situation that you want the confidence to be able to do. Write it down. Then make a pledge to yourself. This will be the decision you make that, for example, 'I *am* going to make the journey on my own', or 'I *am* going to ask for a pay rise.'

State your goal as a positive statement. To increase your chances of achieving your goal, you need to think of it in positive terms. Goals that are framed in such terms as 'mustn't', 'can't', 'won't', 'shouldn't', 'stop', 'lose' or 'quit' are unlikely to motivate you.

Instead of thinking, for example, 'I want to stop working in this crappy horrible job. I want the confidence to just walk out', think, 'I want to get a decent, interesting job. I want the confidence to believe I deserve and can do better.' And instead of thinking, 'I want to ask for a pay rise/discount/apology without feeling really anxious about it', think, 'I want to feel calm and assertive enough to ask for a pay rise/discount/apology.'

Goals framed in positive terms tell you what to do rather than what not to do. Thinking like this creates a positive attitude instead of feelings of struggle and self-doubt.

Visualise it and feel it. See yourself achieving whatever it is you want to do, be or get. Think about how you'll feel when you achieve that goal; how pleased you'll be with yourself and what you've achieved. Return to that image and feeling whenever you feel your confidence slipping.

HAVING REALISTIC EXPECTATIONS

Happiness equals reality minus expectations. —Tom Magliozzi

We each have beliefs and expectations about who we are, who we could and 'should' be and what we could or 'should' be able to do.

Your beliefs and expectations about yourself – your abilities and your worth – may, at one extreme, be high and at the other extreme you could have low expectations. If you have high expectations, when you succeed with what you set out to do or be you'll probably feel pretty good about yourself and your abilities. But your high expectations could mean that you put a lot of pressure on yourself; you believe that you *must* reach your high, idealised standards of perfection and excellence. And if you are unable to meet those high standards, it's likely you'll feel bad about yourself and your abilities, and your confidence and self-esteem may take a hit.

On the other hand, you may have low expectations about your abilities and worth. Although you rarely set yourself up for disappointment, you also rarely step out of your comfort zone and give yourself the opportunity to experience the confidence and self-esteem that go with achieving and succeeding at something.

Somewhere between high and low expectations are *realistic* beliefs and expectations about ourselves, our abilities and our worth. Realistic beliefs and expectations are high enough to present an achievable challenge but low enough to avoid setting yourself up for disappointment. Realistic beliefs and expectations are based on what is actually most possible for you as an individual; what your potential is or what you are actually capable of becoming or achieving.

In Practice

Today you are You, that is truer than true. There is no one alive who is Youer than You. —Dr Seuss

Find your base line; your starting point. In any one situation, what's a realistic expectation for you will be different from what's realistic for someone else. Some people, for example, can expect to feel confident walking into a room full of strangers and spending the rest of the night chatting to anyone and everyone. However, having been to a number of similar social events in the past, you may know that you are more comfortable and confident chatting with a couple of people you already know and leaving early. This, then, is your baseline; your comfort zone. If you want to be more confident to chat to more people at the next social event you go to, you can think what the next realistic, doable step is to build your confidence in that situation next time. In this example, it might simply be to ask a friend to include you in a conversation with one or two new people.

Thinking in terms of a baseline will help determine what, in any one situation, your starting point is and what's a realistic expectation – a realistic next step – for you.

Expect nothing. Whether it's the confidence to join a gym, attend networking events or say what you really think, once you've established your baseline, try to put your expectations – high or low – aside. Take a 'beginner's mind' approach; make a conscious effort to put your judgements, beliefs and expectations aside and, instead, just get started. Just like a scientist setting up an experiment for the purpose of discovering something unknown, just take the next step with no expectations other than to see what happens as a result.

TAKING STEPS TO
BUILD CONFIDENCE

How do you eat an elephant? One bite at a time. —Author unknown

Most people look at mountains and think: 'There's no way I could climb that. That mountain is far too high – it's too challenging.' But anyone who has reached the top of a mountain will tell you that the way they climbed it was to put one foot in front of another. In other words, they took it one step at a time.

The only way to build self-confidence and self-esteem is also one step at a time. What could feel almost impossible in one go becomes a lot more doable as a series of smaller steps. Take too big a leap and, if you fail, you risk knocking yourself back so far that you struggle to get back up again.

If, for example, you wanted to feel confident about going out doing things on your own, eating out at a restaurant alone might feel too daunting and be too big a step. Going to a cafe for a coffee and taking a magazine or paper to read might be far more doable. Once you feel comfortable and confident having done that a couple of times, you are more likely to feel ready/comfortable going to a restaurant on your own.

Remember, confidence is all about believing – convincing yourself – that you *can* do things. Taking a step-by-step approach means you set yourself up for constant successes by achieving small targets along the way. With each step that you achieve, you convince yourself that you *can* do things because each step strengthens your beliefs about what you are capable of and encourages you to believe you can do a bit more with each step.

And, as you learn to develop confidence in one aspect of your life, you'll be able to use the same step-by-step process in other aspects.

In Practice

Get started now. With each step you take, you will grow stronger and stronger, more and more skilled, more and more self-confident, and more and more successful. —Mark Victor Hansen

Remind yourself of what you've already achieved. Think of something you now feel capable and confident doing: your job or an aspect of your job, driving, travelling to new places, playing a sport or a musical instrument, cooking a specific meal or decorating a room. Now think back to when you did it for the first time. Whatever it was, you learned to do it one step at a time and with each step you became more adept, efficient and capable. You became confident in your abilities. You can do it again, in a different situation.

Start from the end. When you lack confidence to do something you probably imagine the worst case scenario; that you'll screw up or fail completely. Instead of worrying and seeing yourself *not* being able to do something, imagine that things turn out well. Now rewind; work it backwards. What would the steps be that led to the situation working out?

Know what your baseline is and take a step forward from there. Decide what that first step could be. For example, you might like to feel more confident about challenging other people's ideas or making suggestions in meetings. You could, therefore, decide, 'I'm comfortable making suggestions, so the first step I'll take from there is to query just one small issue in this afternoon's meeting.'

Keep your mind focused on one step at a time. Tell yourself, 'This is what I'm going to do next' and then just focus on that one step you're taking. If a step feels overwhelming or too difficult or didn't work out, break that step down into smaller steps. Set yourself up for constant successes by achieving small targets along the way and you'll see yourself moving forward and becoming more confident about doing or getting what you want.

HAVING THE COURAGE
TO BE CONFIDENT

You gain strength, courage and confidence by every experience in which you really stop to look fear in the face. —Eleanor Roosevelt

Whenever you don't feel confident about doing something, it's because you don't believe you can do it or that, if you do, it won't turn out well. You feel that what you would like to do, be or have is unlikely to occur.

Imagine, for example, that there was a difficult conversation you needed to have; you wanted the confidence to tell your manager at work that you needed to cut your hours to work a four-day week. Or you wanted to tell a family member you wouldn't be joining them for Christmas, a birthday, an anniversary or a holiday. You're worried about the response you'll get. You think it won't turn out well and that you're unlikely to get what you want.

You need to tap into your courage! Courage gives you the ability to do something *despite* fear, doubt and lack of confidence. In fact, in order to feel confident you have to start with courage. That first step is usually a courageous one.

There is power in doing. When you draw on your courage and take action, confidence will follow. As Christopher Robin said to Winnie the Pooh, 'Always remember: you are braver than you believe, stronger than you seem, and smarter than you think.'

In Practice

Sometimes the biggest act of courage is a small one. —Lauren Raffo

Rather than fight feelings of fear and doubt, accept them. Whether it's courage to do something or say something, acknowledge your fear. Tell yourself 'I'm feeling scared. I'm not sure about this.' Then push past those thoughts and feelings and tell yourself, 'But I *can* do this.' Feel the fear ... and then do it.

Don't overthink it. The more you think about whether you should or shouldn't do or say something, the less likely you are to take that first courageous step. Courage can be prone to leaking, so the longer you wait, the less of it you'll have. Once you've decided to do something, don't wait; do it! Don't wait to feel confident before you do something; do something and confidence will follow.

Decide what is the one thing you'll do first. Do that one thing. Start doing something immediately, without thinking any further and giving your mind time to resist. Once you start doing something, it's easier to continue doing it. Having the courage to initiate that first step will make things happen. And once things are happening, you'll just be dealing with it. So, if you need to have a difficult conversation with someone, decide on your opening line and then just say it. The conversation will go on from there. It may go well or it may not, but at least you've got things moving.

Act 'as if.' Think how you would behave if you were feeling confident. What would you be saying, doing and thinking? Then act 'as if' you were confident. It doesn't mean acting as someone and something you're not; it means acting as someone and something you are aiming to be. And will be soon.

KNOWING YOUR VALUES

Values are like fingerprints. Nobody's are the same, but you leave 'em all over everything you do. —Elvis Presley

We all have values and we each have different values. Maybe you've not given much thought to what your values are, but that doesn't mean you don't have them. Your values encompass what is important to you and what has some worth to you in the way you live, work and relate to other people. You will have personal values that are concerned with how you want to behave and respond to situations; values such as optimism, peace, privacy or security. You'll also have social values – values such as compassion, fairness, cooperation, reliability or honesty – which concern the way you relate to and respond to other people.

What do your values have to do with your confidence? When the decisions you make, what you do and the way you behave and relate to other people match your values, then in a range of situations you can be confident that you are doing the right thing.

Suppose, for example, you didn't have the same pay, rights or privileges at work as some of your colleagues. And suppose your core values included equality and fairness. You can draw on your values of equality and fairness to feel confident – believe you are doing the right thing – in challenging the unfair situation.

Your values are a central part of who you are – and who you want to be. Values can determine your priorities and help you to make decisions with confidence and clarity. If you act according to your values, you can be sure you are acting with integrity. By becoming more aware of these important factors in your life, you can use them as a guide to point you in the right direction, to feel more confident in many situations; to strengthen your beliefs that in any one situation, you *are* doing the right thing.

In Practice

When your values are clear to you, making decisions becomes easier. —Roy E. Disney

Know what is important to you. What do you value? To help you get started, consider these values: compassion, appreciation, fairness, honesty, reliability, dignity, privacy, fun, security, cooperation, belonging. Are any of these important to you? To think more about this, type the words 'list of values' into a search engine for a long list of values that will help you decide which values are important to you. Identify any that have some importance to you, then narrow down your list to six or seven values. These are then your 'core' values; your most important, essential values.

Know that drawing on your values is like wearing the right clothes. When a situation doesn't align with your values – when things feel wrong – it feels uncomfortable and awkward. If you've ever had to dress in a way that wasn't your normal style, you probably felt uncomfortable the entire time. You just didn't feel like you; wearing the 'wrong' clothes zapped your confidence and you felt awkward.

On the other hand, when you dress according to what you feel suits you and works for you, you feel comfortable and believe you look OK. You feel more confident. In the same way, in any one situation where you need to feel confident that you're doing the right thing, know that by drawing on your values you're creating the conditions for confidence.

IDENTIFYING AND ACKNOWLEDGING YOUR STRENGTHS

Don't push your weaknesses. Play with your strengths. —Jennifer Lopez

When our confidence is low, we tend to focus on what we're no good at and the things we don't do well. But there are always going to be things we can't do. Being preoccupied with what's 'wrong' and trying to fix it is an uphill struggle. A more positive approach is to identify what we do well – our strengths – and improve what we are doing right.

Confident people focus on developing their strengths and managing weaknesses. They don't have many more strengths than other people but they have learned to utilise them efficiently in a range of situations.

Your strengths are the personal qualities, abilities, knowledge and skills you already have. Strengths are things that, at the very least, you are competent at – you have sufficient skill, knowledge and experience in. But more likely, your strengths are the things you're good at and that you do well.

When you're doing things that you're capable of and good at, you're doing things that come relatively easily to you. Knowing what your strengths are, you can look for ways and opportunities to use those abilities and qualities and you can also look for ways to build on and develop those strengths.

When it comes to confidence and self-esteem, developing your strengths makes far more sense than trying to become better at things that are not your forte. Focus on what you can do rather than what you cannot.

In Practice

Build upon strengths, and weaknesses will gradually take care of themselves. —Joyce C. Locke

Identify your personal qualities. Put the words 'positive qualities' into a search engine. You'll find words such as patient, reliable, caring, organised, adventurous, persistent and loyal. Tick any that describe you and then narrow it down to the five words that you think most describe you. Then, for each word, write two or three sentences describing how and why you know you have that quality. For example, if you felt that compassion was one of your qualities, you might write, 'I do what I can to help someone if, in some way, they're having a difficult time.' Your example might be 'I recently drove my neighbour to visit his partner in hospital.'

Identify your skills. Think of the skills you have – skills you've acquired through work, study, hobbies and interests.

Ask yourself questions to help you to write about your good qualities and skills. Ask yourself, how has this quality or skill helped me in my work or day-to-day life? What challenges have I overcome by having this quality or skill? How have I helped someone by having this quality or skill?

Feel good about yourself; create your own personal affirmations. By identifying your qualities and skills and writing out how, why and when you have each quality, you are creating your own personal affirmations; positive truths about yourself.

Build on your strengths. Think of something you want more confidence to do. What strengths – what skills and personal qualities – do you already have that could contribute to developing your ability in that area? For example, if you want the confidence to network with others, what relevant strengths do you already have? Maybe you're open-minded and empathic? Draw on those qualities.

MANAGING
FAILINGS AND FOIBLES

*We are all full of weakness and errors; let us mutually pardon each other
our follies – it is the first law of nature.* –Voltaire

Our strengths – personal qualities, skills and abilities – are valuable
assets in developing and maintaining our confidence and self-esteem.
But of course, we've all got weaknesses; we all have imperfections.
Ignoring or denying flaws and faults would be deluded and conceited.
On the other hand, dwelling on failings and foibles doesn't help build
confidence and self-esteem – quite the opposite! Worrying about your
weaknesses and shortcomings is a surefire way to undermine your
confidence and self-esteem – it can discourage you from taking part in
a range of experiences and situations if you believe a weakness or
shortcoming will get in the way. So what to do?

Certainly you can work on your weaknesses to change them. But you can
also change how you think about them. Instead of seeing an aspect of your
character as an inadequacy, start by seeing it in a more objective light.

Take, for example, having a short attention span. Is that a good thing
or a bad thing? It's neither. It's just a thing. What does make it a good
or bad thing, a weakness or a strength, is what you think and believe
about having a short attention span. Usually, people see a short attention span as a weakness. But a short attention span can also be a
strength; it means you can get a series of short tasks and activities done
quickly. You probably find it easy to switch your focus from one task or
activity to another. You may have worked out for yourself that the way
to manage a long, drawn-out job is to break it down into smaller jobs,
take them on one at a time and work in short bursts.

In Practice

Try to look at your weakness and convert it into your strength. That's success. —Zig Ziglar

Identify your weaknesses. In the chapter 'Identifying and acknowledging your strengths' you were asked to put the words 'positive qualities' into a search engine. Look at the list again and this time identify three 'qualities' that you did not pick – that you felt definitely were not you. You might feel, for example, that the words patient, tidy and diplomatic do not apply to you.

Rethink your weaknesses; see them in a positive light. Supposing, for example, you felt that patience was not one of your virtues; that, in fact, you are *im*patient. Is there any way that being impatient could be a good thing? Yes. Impatience comes with its own strengths; you get things done, you're likely to be decisive and you rarely procrastinate or hesitate in taking action.

But does that mean that being indecisive is a weakness? Sure, if you're indecisive you probably find it difficult to commit to a final decision. But a positive aspect of indecisiveness is open-mindedness; you're likely to be receptive to different ideas and possibilities.

Know that time and energy spent berating yourself for your failings and foibles could be better spent looking for the hidden strengths. That's not deluded thinking – it's positive thinking!

THINKING POSITIVELY
AND HAVING HOPE

Optimism is the faith that leads to achievement. Nothing can be done without hope and confidence. —Helen Keller

Positive thinking is a crucial aspect of confidence and self-esteem. Think positively, and you believe and expect that you can do things and that situations are likely to turn out well. Think negatively, on the other hand, and you believe that you can't do things or things won't turn out well. You see and may even look for evidence that supports your belief that you can't or won't be able to do something.

Having a positive outlook does not mean denying the possible challenges and difficulties of a situation. Rather, you acknowledge any potential challenges and then, instead of letting them drag you down into a spiral of negative thinking, you look for the positive aspects and interpretations of a situation.

Supposing, for example, that you had the opportunity to apply for a promotion. If you were thinking negatively, your thoughts might be, 'I probably don't have all the skills and experience needed for this job. No point even applying – they'll see I'd be out of my depth.' But if instead you thought, 'I don't quite have the skills and experience for this job but I can emphasise how willing I am to put in the extra hours to learn,' you would then be thinking positively.

Positive thoughts give you the hope and beliefs that will make it more likely that you will be able to do something. Positive thoughts are confident thoughts!

In Practice

Live your life as if everything is rigged in your favour.
—Arianna Huffington

Think of something you once had to do but were not feeling confident about. For example, your driving test, an interview or a journey you had to make. What thoughts did you have in those situations? Did you think, 'I can't' or 'I won't be able to do it'? Or 'It's all going to go wrong and I'm going to look stupid'? If your thoughts were negative, what thoughts do you now think could have been more positive, helpful and encouraging?

Now think of a specific issue or situation where you'd like to feel more confident. What are your thoughts about it? Ask yourself, 'Does it help my confidence to think like this?' In future, when you catch yourself thinking negatively, remind yourself that negative thinking does not help you feel confident about yourself and your abilities. For example, if you had to travel somewhere new and you were thinking, 'I'm going to get lost. I'll be so stressed. I won't know what to do', in what way is thinking like this helpful? If it prompts you to prepare and plan your journey, all well and good. But if these thoughts just stress you out, they're not helpful.

Have a phrase or word that stops the train of negative thoughts. More often than not, you won't even notice when you're thinking in negative ways. But when you do, simply say, 'Stop!' Or tell yourself 'No, I'm not going there. I'm not thinking like that!' Then refocus your thoughts to more positive, helpful thoughts.

Add the word 'but.' Any time you catch yourself saying a negative sentence, add the word 'but.' This prompts you to follow up with a positive sentence. For example, 'I don't think I can do this. *But* I'll try and if it looks like it's not working out, I'll ask for help.'

SPEAKING WITH CONFIDENCE

Keep your thoughts positive, because your thoughts become your words.
Keep your words positive, because your words become your behavior.
Keep your behavior positive, because your behavior becomes your habits.
Keep your habits positive, because your habits become your values.
Keep your values positive, because your values become your destiny.
—Mahatma Gandhi

'Would you mind if I said something? I just wanted to say that I know I don't know as much as some of the communication experts out there, but, I'm sorry, I'm just wondering if it might be better if we all tried to avoid using minimising language.'

How do you feel about what this person has said? Do you think they sound confident and convincing? Do they sound like they believe in what they're saying? Probably not. By using the words 'would you mind?' 'just,' 'I'm just wondering,' 'I'm sorry,' and 'might,' and stating that 'I may not have as much expertise as others', this person has completely undermined their ability to feel confident and to come across with confidence to the people they were talking to.

The words you use can strengthen or weaken what you say.

How often do you think you might use minimising and qualifying language? The words you use reveal a lot about your levels of confidence; how you view yourself, your choices and decisions, your opinions and judgements and how you view your relationships with others.

It takes some thought and practice, but you can learn to speak with purpose and confidence and show that you believe in what you're saying.

In Practice

If you're presenting yourself with confidence, you can pull off pretty much anything. —Katy Perry

Communicate purposefully. Writing letters, emails and texts provides the perfect opportunity to work on confident language, as you can think about and edit your words before sending. Take this sentence, for example: 'I hope you don't mind but I was wondering if we could meet to discuss the project. I just wanted to share some thoughts, just to check if we agree on the objectives. I'll try to keep it really short, I hope that's OK with you?' Edit out the minimising words so that instead, the message reads 'Could we meet to discuss the project? I wanted to share some thoughts and check if we agree on the objectives. I'll keep it short. Do let me know if that's OK with you.'

Use positive words. Words such as will, can, have, shall, want. Avoid using minimising and qualifying words, such as possibly, just, mustn't and can't. And avoid sentences that begin, 'I hope you don't mind', 'Is it wrong to think ...?' 'I know I shouldn't say this but ...', and 'I may be wrong but ...'

Listen and read. You can learn a lot about confident language just by listening to and reading what other people say. Listen to people talk on the TV and radio. Read what other people say in their emails and texts. Do their words create a positive, confident impression? Listen and look for minimising and qualifying words and phrases. What difference could less negative and more positive words and phrases make? Try and think of positive alternatives. For example, what words would you take out of this sentence, 'Sorry, I don't mean to rush you but I'm wondering if you have made a decision yet?' to make it sound more like a confident question?

HAVING CONFIDENT BODY LANGUAGE

I speak two languages. Body and English. —Mae West

How do you walk into your own kitchen? It's unlikely that you shuffle in with your eyes downcast. You walk with purpose; you walk in with confidence; you believe you belong there.

Think of the last time you were feeling nervous in an interview or at an important meeting. Were you aware of your body language: your posture, facial expressions and gestures? What about a time you were feeling uncomfortable or awkward at a party, a networking event or giving a speech or presentation? Were you looking relaxed and at ease or were you hunched, fidgeting and avoiding eye contact?

Perhaps your mind was too preoccupied with what to do and say to think about how you entered the room, how you were standing or what you were doing with your hands. Maybe, though, you were overly conscious; your hands were trembling and you were convinced that everyone else had noticed too.

Recent research suggests that your posture and other aspects of your body language can actually affect the way your brain functions. Awkward, uncomfortable, uptight and jittery gestures and body language will leave you feeling and thinking the same way.

Carry yourself with confidence, on the other hand, and in a matter of minutes, the chemical balance – the testosterone and cortisol levels in the brain – alters. Your body starts to feel it and your brain starts to believe it. The good news is that you don't have to learn a whole new repertoire of poses, gestures and expressions that feel unnatural or uncomfortable. If you can focus on maintaining just one or two things, the rest of your body and mind will catch up and you will feel more confident and come across as more confident.

In Practice

Our bodies change our minds, and our minds can change our behaviour, and our behaviour can change our outcomes. —Amy Cuddy

In any one situation, if you want to feel calm and more confident – not just appear confident but genuinely feel confident – simply choose to do just one or two of these actions:

- ☐ Stand or sit straight.
- ☐ Keep your head level.
- ☐ Relax your shoulders.
- ☐ Spread your weight evenly on both legs.
- ☐ If sitting, keep your elbows on the arms of your chair (rather than tightly against your sides) or loosely clasped in your lap or on the table in front of you.
- ☐ If standing, keep your hands and arms by your side or loosely clasped in front of you.
- ☐ Make appropriate eye contact.
- ☐ Lower the pitch of your voice and speak more slowly.

You can't control every aspect of your body language. In fact, the harder you try, the more unnatural you are likely to feel. Simply keep your mind on doing one or two of those things and your thoughts, feelings and behaviour will match up. Which one or two actions would you feel comfortable using? Practise using them right now.

PART 2
PERSONAL CONFIDENCE

STEPPING OUT OF YOUR COMFORT ZONE

Life begins at the end of your comfort zone. —Neale Donald Walsh

Comfort happens when things feel good and things feel familiar; you know what to expect, you know what, how and when things will happen and you know what to do and how to do it. You feel at ease and in control. You're in a comfort zone. Being in your comfort zone is a natural state that most people tend towards. It's much easier to remain where you feel comfortable than it is to step out into the unknown.

Staying within your comfort zone could mean, for example, not making a journey or travelling somewhere. Far more comfortable to stay at home. Moving outside this comfort zone – travelling somewhere on your own – is too stressful to even think about!

The thought of stepping out of a comfort zone can make you feel stressed and anxious. But there is another zone – the confidence-building zone.

In any one situation, if you push yourself too hard and too far out of your comfort zone you can find yourself in a panic zone; overwhelmed by anxiety and stress and totally unable to do something. But step just outside a comfort zone into the 'confidence-building zone' and the lower level of anxiety and stress can actually help you to focus, concentrate and achieve things in a controlled, managed way. Although you'll feel challenged, you won't feel too stressed and retreat back into your comfort zone.

Extend your comfort zone and you extend your confidence; you extend your beliefs about what you're capable of in a wide range of situations.

In Practice

Do something uncomfortable today. By stepping out of your box, you don't have to settle for what you are – you get to create who you want to become. —Howard Walstein

Identify your comfort zones. The first step to moving out of your comfort zone is realising that, in a variety of situations, you're in one. It can be so comfy and normal that you don't realise you're in a comfort zone. So think of all the things you do on a regular basis in the same old ways – your daily routine – the time you get up and the time you go to bed, the food and meals you normally eat, the route you take to work, the school run or to the supermarket, to visit friends and family.

Look for opportunities to step outside your comfort zone. Write a list of five things you could do that would move you out of your comfort zone; things that won't involve too much of a stretch. Look at your everyday routines and push yourself to do things a bit differently or a bit more. If, for example, you usually go for a 20-minute run, extend it to 30 minutes. Take a different route to work. Get off the bus or tube one stop earlier and walk. Watch a programme or listen to music you wouldn't normally watch or listen to. Get used to stepping outside your comfort zone. Make it a habit.

Trust yourself; make snap decisions. Now and again, don't overthink it, just step straight out of your comfort zone and do things differently. Allow yourself to do something on impulse. Snap decisions instil a feeling of self-trust. Be spontaneous. If you suddenly feel inclined to do something that's out of your usual routine and takes you out of your comfort zone, just do it.

LETTING GO AND MOVING ON

Life moves on and so should we. –Spencer Johnson

Whether it's arrangements at Christmas that no longer fit in with your plans, classes or a course you want to cut, a job you should've left ages ago or a friendship you want to back out of, too often we remain bound to situations we no longer want to be part of instead of letting go.

There's a number of reasons why you may not have the confidence to let go and move on. For a start, it's difficult to walk away from a situation if you can't see an alternative direction – if you leave the job or course what would you do next? Perhaps letting go and moving on could mean quite a big change in your life. Could you cope? Maybe you know what you want to move on to but you're worried there'll be no going back; you worry that things won't actually be better or turn out well – that, for example, if you leave your job you'll regret it.

Maybe you're worried about other people's reactions; they expect things from you and you might disappoint them or upset them if you do things differently. Perhaps you believe that if you've made a commitment now you should stick with it and put up with any difficulties; the arrangements at Christmas, for example.

Perhaps you tell yourself you've put up with things for so long you might as well carry on; the thought of the time, effort, love or money you've already put into a situation – a relationship, friendship, job or project – will be wasted.

Starting over can be stressful but so is holding on. Holding on is like swimming against the current. It saps your energy – energy that could be better spent on moving on. How do you find the confidence to let go of something that's no longer working for you? It's not just letting go of the situation but also letting go of the beliefs you have that are keeping you trapped in your current situation.

In Practice

Some of us think holding on makes us strong, but sometimes it is letting go. —Herman Hesse

Consider your values; decide what's important to you. Perhaps, for example, you work in a secure job that has specific hours and routines and offers good benefits. But maybe that's no longer in line with your values, and what's important to you now is time with your partner, family or outside interests. Or what's important to you now is more money and opportunities for promotion. Whatever it is, identify your values in that situation and use them as a guide to feel more confident about letting go and moving on. Use your values to point you in the right direction and to strengthen your beliefs that you *are* doing the right thing by letting go.

Know that dwelling on sunk costs – the time, love, money, effort you've already put in – keeps you stuck. Dwelling on sunk costs can fool you into believing you might as well continue putting time, effort or money into someone or something even though it's plainly not doing you any good. Realise that, for a time, the situation and what you put into it was right for you. And that was good. But now it's not; it doesn't line up with your priorities.

Focus on what you have to gain by letting go. Yes, in some situations you may lose out in some way. It's important to acknowledge what you might lose – a longstanding friendship or job security, for example – but rather than dwell on what you might lose, think about what you have to gain by letting go. Know that the best way to let go of the past is to focus on what's important to you now and the foreseeable future.

Get advice. If you can't see an alternative way forward, talk to friends, family and colleagues and ask for their ideas. Seek professional advice if you need information from an expert.

TAKING RISKS

There are risks and costs to action. But they are far less than the long range risks of comfortable inaction. —John F. Kennedy

Starting your own business or skydiving. Telling someone what you really think of them or asking someone out on a date. Renting out a room in your home through Airbnb, travelling in another country on your own or simply going to a café on your own.

We often know what it is we want to do, we simply don't have the confidence to take the plunge. We stay teetering on the edge. We find it difficult to believe that something we want to do will be worth the risk; that things will actually turn out well. You know there's a chance things will go wrong; there are potential hazards and you could lose out in some way. You're not sure that you will be able to handle the responsibility, stress or consequences that come with taking a risk.

But you take a risk every time you get out of bed each morning – as you go about your day there's always the possibility of misfortune! When you *choose* to take risks (as you do when you get out of bed each day) you are making things happen rather than waiting for them to happen to you. Taking a risk can open you up to new ideas, opportunities and experiences. You can discover good things about yourself, your abilities, other people and the world.

Fortuna audaces iuvat! Fortune favours the bold!

In Practice

He who is not courageous enough to take risks will accomplish nothing in life. —Muhammad Ali

Reduce the risk; take a calculated risk. Although fixating on the worst possible scenario can prevent you from taking a risk, it can also help you get prepared; to do what you can to minimise that risk and the possible fall-out. Want to start your own business? Make a business plan. Want to go to a café on your own but worried about feeling conspicious? Take something to read.

Plan how you will handle the worst case scenario. Want to rent out your place through Airbnb but worried about your house being trashed? Want to to ask somone out on a date? What's the risk? What are you worried about? Identify the worst case scenario and then plan how you would deal with that. Think about what would actually happen if your risk didn't pay off and how you would handle it.

If, for example, you wanted to ask someone out on a date, the risk would be that you'd be turned down; you'd feel rejected and embarrassed. So, you might plan to phone a supportive friend after you'd asked the other person out.

Picture everything going well. Imagine that everything will work out. Visualise it going well and keep your mind on the reward. Be realistic about what could go wrong – it's always possible that your risk may not pay off – but it's important to keep the consequences in perspective.

Take a leap of faith. Have courage. Take a deep breath then hold it. The space created by pausing gives you long enough to engage your courage. The second you breathe out, use that moment you have created for yourself to make the leap and take action. Take the risk! Take that first step and let the rest happen from there.

TUNING IN TO YOUR INTUITION

You must train your intuition – you must trust the small voice inside you
which tells you exactly what to say, what to decide. —Ingrid Bergman

How often have you experienced a situation where everything seemed to come together to tell you to definitely do something or to act straight away? Have there also been times when you felt that something was most definitely not right; that things did not add up? Those are times when you've experienced your intuition.

Intuition is that keen and quick insight that tells you something is or isn't right. It's an immediate knowing. It may come as a sudden flash or it may come as a persistent nagging. You don't know why, you can't explain it, you just feel it and you just know it.

So what's the difference between those negative messages we hear ourselves saying when we're not feeling confident such as, 'I'll make a mistake, I won't be able to do it. I'm going to look stupid', and your true inner guidance? If it's intuition, the voice is persistent and direct, but not judgemental. It just says, 'This is wrong.' Or it tells you, 'This is right.' The 'this is it' never feels conflicted or forced. It just feels right.

Intuition doesn't push you into a situation where you feel threatened or unsafe. Quite the opposite; it rings alarm bells when you feel compromised and things are wrong. And it rings celebration bells when things are right.

In Practice

I feel there are two people inside me – me and my intuition. If I go against her, she'll screw me every time, and if I follow her, we get along quite nicely. —Kim Basinger

Know that intuition often comes and goes in a flash. If you're aware of something – it might be a glimpse of something happening, a brief passing look from someone else or a momentary sound – that makes you think that things aren't right, focus. Don't allow anything else to divert your attention.

When intuition is coming through as a constant nagging, be alert for a combination of signals. So often, intuitive messages are drowned out by all the other internal and external noise and activity that's going on in and around you. If you experience a low-level but persistent feeling that all is not right, tune in to what that combination of signals might be telling you.

As well as being aware of external things happening, trusting your intuition also means being aware of the information your senses are communicating to you; what your ears, eyes, nose, sense of taste, sense of touch and physical sensations are telling you. That 'sixth sense' is actually all the information from your five senses coming together. When all the information your senses are receiving does add up, your intuition is coming through loud and clear.

Train your intuition. All your senses are constantly picking up information from the world around you. Being more aware of your environment – the sights, sounds, smells, etc. – on an everyday basis will alert you when things are different; when things aren't right. Notice what's normal *and* what's new in familiar situations. Notice smells, sights and sounds. Then, when you notice things being out of place or unusual, you will recognise your intuition is warning you.

HAVING A CONFIDENT BODY IMAGE

There is no wrong way to have a body. —Glenn Marla

How do you feel about your body? Are you pleased with the body you have or are you often disappointed? Feeling bad about the way you look can seriously undermine your confidence and self-esteem.

Sure, it can be hard not to compare yourself unfavourably to the body shapes that surround you. But often, people who have what many of us would think of as an ideal body are just as likely to be dissatisfied with their body and unhappy about their looks as the rest of us. A person can work at their body until every inch of it is toned, tanned, firm and fat-free, but if you still don't believe that you look good, then it doesn't count for much!

So often, how we see ourselves is not a reality; it's an illusion. You may, for example, not only feel fatter after eating a slice of cake, you're often convinced that you *are* fatter when in fact you couldn't possibly look any different!

It isn't so much down to what your body looks like but how you feel about it that counts. Your body image is just your *idea* of what you think your body 'should' and does look like.

How can you become more body confident? Certainly not by starving yourself, sweating and pummelling your body into the shape you think it 'should' be. Instead, re-frame the way you view, think and talk about your body.

In Practice

No body is perfect. I just don't believe in perfection. But I do believe in saying, 'This is who I am and look at me not being perfect!' I'm proud of that. —Kate Winslet

Avoid getting into, 'I hate my upper arms/neck/thighs/teeth/stomach' conversations with other people. Getting caught up in a conversation about the way someone else looks, whether they've put on weight, they think their arms are flabby, their nose is too big, their face is too lined and so on, inevitably affects the way you view your own body. Before you know it, you're falling into competitive self-criticism; as soon as your friend mentions a flaw, you trump it with one of yours. The next time a friend brings up their body hang-up, change the conversation to focus on your positives. Each come up with three body positives, for yourself and for each other. That way you can both feel better.

Avoid tabloid and gossip media that constantly shame celebrities' bodies. 'The eyes of others are our prisons; their thoughts our cages,' Virginia Woolf once wrote. She's right.

Shift your focus from what your body looks like to what it can do. When you think about yourself in terms of what your body can do, you start to view your body in a very different way; a positive way. Appreciate that every day your body is working for you; walking, running, lifting and holding, writing, talking, cutting, chopping and stirring. The list is endless.

Increase your body's potential. Of course we've all got different levels of physical ability. But whatever your ability, you can challenge your body to a new activity or a creative skill – like drawing, painting or crafts – or physical exercise like a dance class, hiking, cycling or climbing.

Look after and reward your body. Make an effort to take care of your body in the ways that you know make you feel good. For you, that might mean a great haircut, a manicure, a relaxing bath ... whatever it is that makes you feel good about your body.

CHANGING YOUR JOB OR CAREER

You are never too old to set another goal or to dream a new dream. —C.S. Lewis

Whatever it is you do for a job, does something else appeal to you? Do you find yourself increasingly drawn to something new? Perhaps those aspects of your job and career you once enjoyed have disappeared through changes that have taken place in your job or your life. You've lost interest and become disillusioned and now there's something else you wish you were doing instead.

Maybe there's a job within your current company – you work in finance for a publisher but have become interested in working as an editor. Or perhaps you want a complete change – from working in town planning to acting, fashion design to conservation, running a cafe instead of teaching or being a plasterer instead of a social worker.

What's stopping you? Perhaps a career change will mean a drop in earnings or you're worried it will take too long to retrain. Maybe you're concerned that other people – family, colleagues and friends – will think you're mad to give up your job and career for the uncertainty of something new.

Perhaps you simply lack confidence to break out of your current situation. You're wondering if your interest in a different career is just a phase. If you do make the change, how will you know you're doing the right thing? What if it doesn't work out?

In Practice

If you do not change direction you may end up where you're heading. —Lao Tzu

Explore your work values and find out what's important to you in a job or career. When you enjoy your job, work or career and you're engaged in what you're doing, you are using your interests, skills and strengths. But, just as importantly, your work matches your values. Your work values are the things that are important to you in the work you do; they give purpose and meaning to the work you do. Here are examples of work values: helping others, prestige and status, job security, teamwork, working on your own, being appreciated, high pay, leadership and influence, variety, challenge, creativity, routine and procedure. Which of these values are important to you? Type 'work values' into a search engine for a more comprehensive list that will help you identify your work values.

Does your work or career reflect your values? If, for example, fun, teamwork and adventure are important to you, think about whether or not they are aspects of the work or career that appeals to you.

Making a career change is an opportunity to think about your values and determine what matters most to you. Take the time you need to determine what's most important to you in your career and lifestyle.

If you are pursuing a job or career that aligns with what you value, you may need to make sacrifices in terms of money, time etc. but, if you really want to make that change, when you know that the career or job matches your values, you can be confident that you are doing the right thing.

Talk to people who are in the line of work you're interested in. And talk to people who have successfully changed career direction; who have swapped accountancy for being a horse riding instructor or journalism for marketing. Ask around or read about them.

CALMING CONFIDENCE

Calm mind brings inner strength and self confidence. And that's very good for health. —Dalai Lama

The clock is ticking. Your heart is racing. Everyone's counting on you. Which wire should you cut? Get a grip. Stay focused. Keep calm.

OK, so you might never be called on to defuse a bomb. But situations such as job interviews, speaking in front of a group and complaining about faulty goods or poor service can be every bit as stressful if you're not used to dealing with them. Whatever the situation, when the pressure is on you can feel yourself getting flustered. You need the assurance that comes with quiet, calm confidence.

The more confident you are, the more calm and relaxed you are, and the more calm and relaxed you are, the easier it is for you to remain confident. But if you have no experience of moving your mind to a calmer place it can feel impossible to gather yourself; to take a step back so that you can you think clearly and stay calm, composed and focused. How do you turn tension to tranquility? Building the skill beforehand can be helpful for when difficult situations come up.

In Practice

Self-confidence comes from a steady sense of inner calm, an easy, unhurried bearing. —Confucius

Breathe. When a challenge arises, bring your attention to your breathing. Mindful breathing provides a focal point for your mind that can help slow everything down, calm your mind and body and anchor you.

Focusing on your breathing is a simple thing you can do or practise anywhere, anytime.

Take a deep breath. Then take one more. Then breathe normally; just focus on breathing in ... then breathing out. Place one hand on your chest and feel your breath moving into and out of your body. Notice the natural rhythm. No doubt you will notice thoughts arising as you breathe. Just allow them to come and go and return your focus and attention to your breathing.

There are a number of other ways you can focus on your breath. The '4-7-8 breathing technique' is useful. Put 'breathing exercises' into a search engine to find the 4-7-8 and other breathing techniques. Try out a few and see which is the most doable for you. Which breathing technique you use is not as important as just remembering to use one of them when you need to feel calm and collected.

Try and practise a mindful breathing technique for a minute or two each day. It might be first thing in the morning, on the journey to work, with a cup of tea or coffee, at lunch or before you go to sleep at night.

Practise slowing down. Whatever you do next, slow it down by 25 percent. Whether it's working on the computer, making a cup of tea or cleaning the kitchen, take your time; do those things more slowly, more completely and with more concentration. Make your actions deliberate, not rushed and random.

MAKING CONFIDENT DECISIONS

Some persons are very decisive when it comes to avoiding
decisions. —Brendan Francis

Whether to take this job or that job, to live here or move there, to study this subject or that subject, to order one thing from the menu or another, you have to make a decision. So, what's it going to be? Have you made up your mind? You can't decide?

When you find it difficult to make a decision it's often because you don't believe – you're not confident – that you'll definitely be making the 'right' choice and the 'best' decision. You're worried about the consequences of a 'wrong' decision.

Delegating decisions because you know someone else is better qualified, has more knowledge or expertise about a situation is often a sensible, practical way forward. But passing the buck because you don't want to take the blame for a 'wrong' choice is unfair to other people and doesn't give you the opportunity to make confident decisions.

Perhaps, though, you don't need anyone else to make decisions for you – you prefer to think things through for yourself. But too often you spend ages agonising over the pros and cons of each option; you overthink the situation. Sometimes you're so stuck you make no decision. And yet making no decision is still a decision; you've made a decision not to do anything.

Even if you do make a final choice, you might start wondering if it was the right decision. And actually, now you know it was the wrong one. Probably. At least you think it might be. Or perhaps not.

What to do? How do you accept uncertainty and make a choice despite possible unknowns?

In Practice

There are people who can come to no decision on any matter without first having slept over it. This is all very well; but cases may occur where on this plan you risk being captured, bed and all. —Georg Christoph Lichtenberg

Make a well-informed decision; a decision based on your aims and values. In any one situation where you have to make an important decision – moving home or job, leaving a relationship or friendship – identify your values, what's important to you, and your aims, what you're hoping to achieve. Identifying your values and aims narrows your choices so that you pay attention to relevant factors – what's important to you in this situation – not irrelevant ones.

Have courage. Accept uncertainty; make a choice despite possible unknowns. Know there is no 'right' or 'wrong' decision. When you're finding it difficult to make a decision, for each option ask yourself, 'What's the worst that can happen? How might I deal with that?' Know that you can make a choice and if things don't work out you will already have thought of what to do to manage what happens.

Learn from a 'wrong' decision. Instead of berating yourself, choose to learn from the situation so that you can make a 'better' decision next time. Whether you choose to drive or get the train, or you decide on this job or career or that job or career, if it doesn't work out, can you think about what you learned from that situation that could inform a similar decision next time? Each time you learn from a situation, you build your confidence to deal with a similar situation next time around.

Do make a well-informed decision, but know that the pursuit of more information can be a way of putting off a decision. Don't wait until conditions are perfect, get started now. If new information comes to light after you have made your decision, if necessary, you can alter your course then.

CHANGING YOUR MIND

If you never change your mind, why have one? —Edward De Bono

How often do you change your mind? Possibly more than you realise. It could've been this morning when you decided to eat toast instead of cereal. Then, as you set off to work you decided not to take an umbrella with you. But when you stepped outside the front door and saw the dark clouds, you changed your mind. And perhaps last night, rather than going out to the pub you chose to stay in and watch a film instead.

But when it comes to bigger issues – deciding that actually, you don't want to buy or rent that flat after all, you don't want the job or place at university you've accepted, or to go on holiday with your friends – you struggle to change course.

Politicians usually face a great deal of scorn when they change their minds about an issue. Their opponents accuse them of making a U turn and declare that the person is inconsistent, weak and unreliable. The message we then pick up is that changing one's mind is a negative thing; it suggests weakness and a lack of confidence. Not so!

We've all found ourselves in situations where we've needed to change our minds; maybe it was a time when you realised you'd jumped ahead of yourself and made a decision too quickly. Or what you thought you wanted to do doesn't now seem such a good idea after all; you realise it's not the right decision after all. Perhaps your circumstances have changed and you have new options. It could be that what you've now decided to do is more in line with your abilities, is more realistic and achievable for you. Maybe you've simply had a change of heart; your feelings about a situation have changed.

You may feel embarrassed that you've got to explain your change of mind to friends, family or colleagues, but having a few uncomfortable conversations is a small price to pay for making the right choice.

In Practice

If you can change your mind you can change your
life. —William James

Tune in to your intuition. It may come as a sudden flash – an immediate knowing – or it may come as a persistent nagging that you need to change course; that there's a better option. Either way, take notice – let your intuition prompt you to think how what you now want aligns with your values and goals. When your hunches and gut feelings match up with your values, aims, strengths etc., you can be confident that your change of mind is right for you.

Be clear with yourself about the reason or reasons you've changed your mind. Maybe you no longer want to be a vegetarian; you've decided that actually you'd denied yourself something you enjoyed, you didn't need to give up meat, just eat far less of it. Or the job offer you accepted; upon reflection you realise you wouldn't be able to cope with the commute. Whatever the reason, acknowledge it and own it.

Think positive. Instead of seeing yourself as weak and indecisive, see yourself as open-minded, flexible and able to change and adapt according to new information and circumstances. Rather than thinking you've changed your mind, see it as having made a *new decision*.

If someone else is going to be worse off as a result of you changing your mind, tell them as soon as you can. Apologise. Say what, if anything, you can do to compensate.

Have courage. Lots of people wish they had the courage to change course like you. Your boldness in changing direction could inspire others to do the same.

RETURNING TO LEARN

Live as if you were to die tomorrow. Learn as if you were to live forever.
—Mahatma Gandhi

Very young children appear to find it easy to learn. They watch and copy, ask questions, try things out, make mistakes and try again. They don't tell themselves they can't learn; if they fall down they just get back up and start again. It doesn't occur to them that they can't learn; that they can't understand something or that they can't increase their knowledge and skills. They're confident about learning – they believe they *can* learn.

Is there something you'd like to learn? Maybe you left school years ago and you'd like to return to learn; you're thinking about going to college or university. What's stopping you? Are you doubting your ability to learn? If you haven't studied for a long time maybe you think you're too old; that you've left it too late. Or if you didn't do well at school, if past experiences of learning weren't good, maybe you think you're not clever enough; that you don't have the ability or skills to learn and that you're not intelligent enough.

Perhaps you compare yourself with others who you think are cleverer than you. More likely, they're just more confident. Confidence plays a big part in learning. You can start to strengthen your beliefs in your ability to learn by discovering how you learn best.

In Practice

You are braver than you believe, stronger than you seem, and smarter than you think. —A.A. Milne

Identify how you learn best. Write down three things you've learnt in the past. For example, a language, a musical instrument, to swim, to drive, to use technical equipment, to build or make something, to cook or to decorate. For each thing, how did you learn it? Was it by reading instructions? By watching a YouTube video? Did a teacher, a friend or a colleague show you? Write down how you learnt each of those three things.

Next, write down what helped you to learn each thing. Was it clear instructions? Was it because you practised what you were learning over and over again? Was it a good teacher? If so, what did they do that helped?

Identify your learning styles. Are you a reflective learner, an active learner or a pragmatic learner? To find out, Google 'Honey and Mumford learning questionnaire.' Then, find out if you are a visual learner or a kinaesthetic learner. Google 'audio visual kinaesthetic learning quiz.'

Keep in mind that confident learners know they learn best when they are learning in ways that work best for them. How do you learn best? What helps you to learn? What are your strengths as a learner? We've all got preferred ways of learning. When you understand what yours are, you can devise ways of learning that work best for you; you take responsibility for your own learning.

MAKING MISTAKES

A life spent making mistakes is not only more honourable, but more
useful than a life spent doing nothing. —George Bernard Shaw

Do you like making mistakes? Probably not. There's nothing worse than that sinking feeling when you realise you've slipped up and made a mistake. You feel awkward and annoyed with yourself. And if your mistake was in front of other people, you probably feel embarrassed or even ashamed.

Maybe though, there's something you want to do or something you're interested in learning; a language or a musical instrument. Perhaps you want to join a choir, take dance lessons or learn magic tricks. Or someone has asked you to take on a new project at work. Perhaps you don't have the confidence to give it a go in case you make mistakes.

It's true that when you attempt something new and you are inexperienced at something it's likely you'll make mistakes, so it's no wonder that you might greet new challenges with little enthusiasm. But not doing something for fear of making a mistake is ... well, it's a mistake. If you already have low self-esteem and confidence, if you avoid taking up new interests or taking on new things you never give yourself the chance to develop a new skill. You don't give yourself the opportunity to feel good about yourself for having achieved something new.

Think of something you now feel capable and confident doing, like driving a car. Almost certainly you will have made mistakes. But you learnt from those mistakes; you saw where you went wrong and practised till you got it right; became more adept, efficient and capable. At some point, you no longer made mistakes; you became confident in your abilities and pleased with yourself.

You've learnt new skills before and dealt with the mistakes before. You can do so again.

In Practice

Failure is instructive. The person who really thinks learns quite as much from his failures as from his successes. —John Dewey

Allow yourself to make mistakes. Start anything new by telling yourself, 'I'm not going to be good at this right away, I'm going to make mistakes and that's OK. Making mistakes is not going to put me off.'

Think about what you are doing in terms of learning and improving. All the time you're trying to do things really well and avoid mistakes you put pressure on yourself. And when you're feeling pressured and stressed you're actually more likely to make mistakes. On the other hand, when you simply get on with a task with a view to learning and improving, you're calmer and more able to concentrate. An example of this is the difference between driving lessons and a driving test. When you're having a driving lesson you're simply focused on learning and improving. But typically, when you take your test, you're worrying about your driving and trying to avoid mistakes. The pressure to do well and avoid mistakes can result in many more mistakes.

Keep your mind focused on one step at a time. Tell yourself, 'This is what I'm going to do next' and then just focus on that one step you're taking. Set yourself up for constant successes by achieving small targets along the way and you'll see yourself moving forward.

Learn from mistakes. You can't change mistakes, but you can choose how to respond to them. The best way to handle a mistake is to learn from it. So you're learning French and said the wrong thing. So what? Just ask what the right way is to say it.

Confident people take mistakes in their stride – they know that being able to do anything with confidence involves making mistakes; they see mistakes as something to learn from as they keep progressing.

COPING WITH CHANGE

If nothing ever changed, there'd be no butterflies. —Author unknown

Do you suffer from metathesiophobia? Never heard the word? Turns out that metathesiophobia is the fear of making changes. The origin of the word 'meta' is Greek, meaning 'after' and 'change.' 'Thes' is Latin for 'setting' and phobia is Greek for 'fear.'

Mostly, we take the changes that happen in our stride – changing the clocks in autumn and spring, the changes in the weather, the time a favourite TV programme is scheduled or your team is playing, a change in the menu at a favourite restaurant or a change in where the milk is stocked in your local shop.

But facing a more serious change – a major staff reshuffle or changes in procedures at work, redundancy, moving home, good friends or close family moving away – can leave you feeling apprehensive, threatened and vulnerable.

The prospect of change can mean you're facing an uncertain future, not knowing what to expect and often assuming the worst. You don't feel confident – you don't believe – you'll be able to adapt and cope with the change in circumstances or that things will work out well.

Often, we can't control changes or stop them from happening. But we can control how we respond to change. Rather than see it as a bad thing and resist change, you need to face change with confidence; with the belief that you *can* cope.

In Practice

Welcome change as the rule but not as the ruler. —Denis Waitley

Get informed. If you're currently facing a change, find out what you can about what the changes will involve. Ask questions and get information about the change.

Write a list of all the negative things that you think a change will bring. Uncertainty and loss? What else? It's important to acknowledge the negative aspects – don't ignore or deny the challenges and difficult emotions that changes bring.

Draw on your strengths. Once you've identified the potential difficulties, gain an element of control; prepare to manage change by drawing on your strengths. What skills, abilities and knowledge do you have that you can use to manage the challenges that the change will bring?

Have positive beliefs and expectations. Now write down the positive things, such as new opportunities, that change brings. Acknowledge and do what you can to prepare for the negative aspects of a change. Then choose to focus on the positive aspects.

Practise making changes and see that you can adapt. Choosing to break a routine way of doing things on a regular basis can be an effective tactic for coping with the inevitable changes that will occur in your life. Drive, walk or cycle a different route to somewhere you regularly go. You could even take a different route from your normal one around the supermarket. Move the clock or the wastepaper bin to a different place in the room. See how long it takes you to stop looking in the wrong place for the time or throw rubbish on the floor. What could you do? Start today. Train yourself to manage change.

COPING WITH SETBACKS TO YOUR CONFIDENCE

Winners never suffer defeat, just setbacks on their way to victory. —Orrin Woodward

It's easy to feel confident and good about yourself when things are going well in your life. The real challenge comes when something happens that severely knocks your confidence and self-esteem. Losing your job or getting turned down for a place on a course or a job can set you back. So can financial difficulties, health problems, injury or a bereavement. If someone else lets you down badly, cheats on you or bullies you, you'll probably suffer a setback to your confidence and self-esteem; you doubt yourself, your abilities, your worth and your place in the world.

When life knocks you down, it can be tempting to just lie there. It's a natural response; feelings of sadness and disappointment are intended to slow you down and give you time to take in and adjust to what's happened.

At some point, though, you'll need to move on. It's not easy to bounce back to where you were, but the longer you allow your thoughts to brood on what did or didn't happen, the more likely your confidence and self-esteem will ebb away even further.

In Practice

Turn a setback into a comeback. —Author unknown

Make a decision that you are going to bounce back. At some point after you've taken in and adjusted to what happened, you need to steer your mind in a positive direction and rebuild your confidence and self-esteem.

Look for what you can learn from the setback. Learning from a setback involves reflecting on what happened, what went wrong, working out what, if anything, needs to change and what to do to avoid similar disappointments and setbacks in the future.

As the interviewer Zane Lowe said to Kanye West – 'You win or you learn, right?' Sports participants know that whenever they or their team lose they can't dwell on the setback for long. Instead, they identify what went wrong and what they can learn from what happened. They then move on to think about the next game or race and what they need to do to get back on form. In order to rebuild your confidence and self-esteem you must do the same; make a decision that you are going to bounce back. It won't happen automatically, you have to make an effort.

Rebuild your confidence step by step. In a situation where you want to recover from a setback to your confidence, first think about what you *do* feel comfortable and capable of doing. This is your starting point. Now think of something you can do – one small step you can take that will enable you to achieve and feel good about yourself. If, for example, you were trying to recover your confidence to drive after a car accident, you might simply start by driving round the block. Then each day, drive a bit farther. Know that small wins help you feel in control, think positively and feel good about yourself. Small wins are the building blocks of confidence.

TRAVELLING WITH CONFIDENCE

*The world is a book, and those who do not travel read only one
page. —Saint Augustine*

Planes, trains and automobiles. And buses and taxis. Whatever the mode
of transport, travel is not everyone's idea of fun. It's not difficult to
imagine a range of potential scenarios: missing your flight, getting on
the wrong train, missing the stop. What if you miss the last bus or train
home? Supposing you get stranded? Travelling on busy roads and motor-
ways, finding your way around a busy city and getting lost. Traffic jams
and delays. Worrying about your car breaking down.

It's no wonder you might not feel confident about making a journey and
travelling somewhere. A travel fear may be stopping you in your tracks.
Quite literally. But stay where you are and you're missing out; there are
places to go, things to see and people to meet. Friends and family, films
and festivals, sunsets and night skies waiting for you.

As Mark Twain once wrote, 'Twenty years from now you will be more
disappointed by the things you didn't do than by the ones you did do.
So throw off the bowlines, sail away from the safe harbor. Catch the
trade winds in your sails. Explore. Dream. Discover.'

In Practice

Man cannot discover new oceans unless he has the courage to lose sight of the shore. —André Gide

Plan and prepare your journey. Check out the bus or train stops to your destination, make a note of them and cross each one off as you reach it. Or use Google maps, Galileo or Viewfinder apps and follow your route on the train. Download the National Rail app to help plan your train journey. You can even get a 'wake me up' alarm which will alert you when it's your stop (you can set it to give a 1, 5 or 10-minute warning).

Break it down. If you have a four-hour car journey, break it down into four shorter journeys. After an hour, stop for coffee, an hour later for lunch and an hour later for another coffee.

Tell a friend. Let someone know that you're worried about making the journey and you want to know that they'll be available if you need to call for reassurance.

Nervous about finding your way round the airport? Familiarise yourself with the airport plan on the airport's website. You can also download maps of major train stations.

Check departure times of last buses or trains. Aim to get the one before that.

Worried about getting stranded? As long as you have a mobile phone and a credit card, you can be confident that no matter what happens you'll be able to stay in a hotel or get home again with another bus, train or taxi.

Make the journey enjoyable. Take something extra nice to eat, read, listen to or watch to occupy your time.

RETURNING TO WORK

There is nothing like returning to a place that remains unchanged to find the ways in which you yourself have altered. —Nelson Mandela

Returning to work after an extended break is not always easy whatever the reason – illness, redundancy, maternity leave, parenting or being a carer – and whether it's been 12 months or more than a decade, going back to work can be a daunting prospect.

There's a number of reasons why you may not be feeling confident about returning to work. Perhaps you think you'll have forgotten what you used to know. Maybe you're not sure if you'll be able to learn new procedures and policies. Technology has moved on and you're not sure how well you will adapt and adjust. Or maybe you're worried about whether or not you'll be able to balance work with your personal commitments.

It could be that you're worried about explaining a gap in your working life to potential employers; you've created a negative picture of yourself, telling yourself that you've lost skills and you'll be out of your depth and you think employers will see things the same way. But that's not true! Well, it's only true if that's how you present yourself.

Even though you may feel nervous about it, you *can* get back in the saddle!

In Practice

The moment you doubt whether you can fly, you cease forever to be able to do it. —J.M. Barrie

Focus on your strengths. If you've been off work for a while, there might be a gap in your CV but this is something every employer has come across. You don't need to go into uncomfortable details, just a simple 'caring for parent/partner/children' or 'break after redundancy' and a *brief* explanation will help employers understand the gap. What's of interest to a potential employer are your past and current skills, qualifications and experience that are relevant to the job. They are all still valid, so focus on those.

Get support. There's plenty of advice online to help you write your CV. Google 'How to write your CV' for some useful advice.

Take steps to build confidence. If you're returning to your last job, maybe you can start by working fewer hours for the first few weeks? If you're looking for a new job, maybe you can start by getting a temp or part-time job?

Are you in a position to do some voluntary work? Volunteering is a less-pressured way of getting back into working life. Helping other people and making a contribution in some way is great for your confidence and self-esteem. Voluntary work builds your network and may even lead to a permanent role. It will also enhance applications for jobs if the voluntary work role gives you experience of using the skills required for future paid work.

Brush up your knowledge and skills. Or learn something new related to the work you're interested in. There are a number of ways to become more familiar with new technology and other skills. Find online or in-class courses in your area via nationalcareersservice .direct.gov.uk or http://www.hotcourses.com/ or you could ask a friend or colleague to teach you what you need to learn.

PART 3
SOCIAL CONFIDENCE

MAKING SMALL TALK

You can make more friends in two months by becoming interested in other people than you can in two years by trying to get other people interested in you. —Dale Carnegie

Small talk doesn't come easily to all of us. Whether it's in a pub or club, at parties or weddings, conferences or meetings or simply in the queue for coffee or at the bus stop, there's a number of places and occasions when small talk can be a big challenge.

Maybe you think small talk is shallow or boring and that there's more to life than talking about the weather; if it's sleet, snow or rain and how cold it is. Or perhaps you find the idea of having to make social chit chat alarming; you do what you can to avoid occasions where you might be required to make small talk with people you hardly know.

Small talk can be the start of something; many friendships and relationships have started with a discussion about the weather or the price of fish. But small talk is also simply about being civil, courteous and considerate; to come across as an approachable, friendly person who is open to exchanging a few pleasantries.

Approach small talk with the belief that you'll have nothing to say and that it's going to be awkward and it probably will be. Adjust your beliefs and expectations; you don't have to impress, you don't have to be brilliant, just nice. Smile, be interested, ask questions, take a genuine interest in the other person and say something about yourself.

In Practice

Here's my trick for talking to people: numbers! Ask them questions to which the answer is a number. There's always an answer. 'How long have you lived here? What time do you start work? When did you do that?' —Jerry Seinfeld

Have courage; make the first move. If you're at a party, convention or any other social gathering, be bold. Choose a person who seems approachable – someone standing by themselves is a good bet – then just make eye contact, smile and say, 'Hi, I'm ...' You don't need to have the perfect opening questions. Just start with the usual questions: 'What do you do?' 'How do you know Paulo?' 'Have you been here before?' but you do need to be interested in and follow up on their answers.

Comment or ask their opinion on something that both you and the other person are experiencing; where you're both at and what's around you. For example, say 'I really love this restaurant.' It's likely they'll ask you why, which opens up another opportunity for conversation. And if they don't, ask what they think of the place.

Imagine that the other person is already your friend. It can help you feel more relaxed and comfortable.

Conversations dry up when you look for the 'right' things to say. If you feel like talking about the ice-cream you had for breakfast, do that. If you follow it up by asking, 'What's the weirdest thing you've had for breakfast?' you've opened up the conversation. Say something about a book you're reading, a blog or website you've found interesting. What about a film you've recently seen, something funny or interesting you heard on the news. An app you can't live without. Did you lose your keys or find £10? Tell the other person then ask if they've ever done the same.

Practise making small talk. Get used to starting a conversation and talking to people you don't know. Talk with people who work at a shop or café – anyone who works with the public can be easy to chat to because they're used to people making small talk.

GIVING AND TAKING COMPLIMENTS

Marge, you're as pretty as Princess Leia and as smart as Yoda. —Homer Simpson

If someone gives you a compliment, do you accept it and allow it to make you feel good? Or, not wanting to appear immodest, do you brush it off? Perhaps someone's compliment or praise doesn't line up with how you see yourself; you're more comfortable sticking with your own negative beliefs about yourself than accepting that someone else's positive remarks about you are true.

But not only does rejecting praise not serve you well, it's rude; you're telling the other person that they're wrong. When someone gives you a compliment it's the same as if they were giving you a gift. Therefore, if you reject the compliment it's like rejecting and refusing to accept a gift. And that's not nice, is it?

A more positive response – one that's gracious and helps you to feel good about yourself – is to acknowledge and accept a compliment, praise or appreciation.

Not only are compliments good for you to receive, they're good for you to give, too; an opportunity to look for the best in others and put your appreciation in words.

Whether you praise a colleague, show appreciation to a friend or family member or say thanks to a company or individual for good service, your compliment will let the other person know that their actions have been noticed and help them feel good about themselves and their abilities. Not only can it brighten someone's day, a compliment or praise can also enhance your own well-being; if the people around you feel good, you'll feel good too. Instant karma!

In Practice

I can live for two months on a good compliment. —Mark Twain

Accept compliments. Think of accepting a compliment as an exercise in self-esteem and confidence. Decide to accept what the person is saying as a real possibility; that it *is* possible that you are considerate, funny or kind. Accept the compliment as legitimate. By accepting a compliment, you're acknowledging something positive about yourself; that you do have worth and value.

Believe the other person; they're being nice and they're being genuine. Be gracious and accept a compliment in the same way you would accept a gift; just say 'thank you.' And if you say more than that, make sure it's positive; say, 'How nice, thank you.' Or, 'Thank you. I really appreciate you telling me.'

Don't respond with a negative remark. If someone says, 'I love your jacket, that colour looks great on you.' Don't respond with, 'Thanks, but I think it looks old fashioned.' And don't contradict them. Don't say, 'No, it doesn't.'

Give compliments. Look for ways to compliment people for their actions. Acknowledge personal qualities or special efforts; a person's concern and patience or the extra time they put into something. If what they've done has had a positive effect on you, tell them, 'Your concern helped me feel better,' or, 'You explained it so well. Now I understand how to ...'

Notice the work someone does. It could be someone who serves you in a shop or café. Make a positive comment.

Take a look around and see who you can pay a compliment to today. If you like something someone has done, has made, is wearing etc., don't keep it to yourself. Tell them.

NETWORKING WITH CONFIDENCE

If you want to go fast, go alone. If you want to go far, go with others.
—African proverb

Someone once said that the opposite of networking is not working. But whether it's for professional or social reasons, networking can introduce you to a world of new contacts and new opportunities. Networking is about making contacts and connections, exchanging interests and ideas, information and experience.

As well as time and effort, it takes confidence to network; you need to believe that you have something to contribute, that people will be interested in what you have to offer and will genuinely want to offer you something – ideas, information, contacts etc. – in return.

Of course, there's never been a better time to network; technology has made networking easier and quicker. With only a person's name, you can Google them and find their LinkedIn profile, their Facebook information and, if they tweet, their Twitter stream. None the less, online networking doesn't detract from the importance of networking in person with other people. If you want to get ahead, you do need to get out there.

It may have you wanting to run for the hills but there are other people out there who are open to mutually beneficial connections. Get out there and meet them!

In Practice

Networking is more about farming than it is about hunting. It's about cultivating relationships. —Ivan Misner

Have a purpose. If you're going to a conference, meeting or networking event, before you go, find out who else is going. Do your homework on any specific people you would like to meet. What would you like to talk to them about? What might you have in the way of ideas, information or resources that you could offer the people you'd like to meet?

Think through how you could help them and vice versa. Prepare some questions in advance that can start a conversation with anyone you happen to encounter. Think about what you might want to learn from them.

Have an idea about how you're going to introduce yourself to people. Know how to talk succinctly, without rambling about what you do or make, your product or the services you offer.

For any one networking event, set a goal for yourself. You might aim to meet two or three people, who would be specifically interested in what you have to offer, show or sell. Or you might want to find someone who has a particular skill or knowledge about something. Your aim might be to do nothing more than meet a number of people and simply find out who they are, what they do and who they know.

Networking happens one person at a time. Aim to talk one-on-one rather than in groups. If you do join a group, be bold – approach the group, introduce yourself and ask, 'Could I join your conversation?'

Follow up. If you say you'll be in touch, that you'll send them some information, then do. Make sure you do what you said you would. And if, in future, you come across something that might be of interest to them, do make contact – keep the connection going.

SPEAKING UP

*What is the source of our first suffering? It lies in the fact that we
hesitated to speak. It was born in the moment when we accumulated
silent things within us.* —Gaston Bachelard

Speaking up means saying what you're thinking; it's expressing your
ideas and opinions. But in a range of situations, it can take quite a bit
of confidence to speak up and put your idea, suggestion or observation
forward; to believe that what you have to say is worth saying.

Supposing, for example, you're in a meeting and you have an idea about
how to tackle a problem with a project you're all working on. The voice
in your head is saying, 'Tell them! Tell them your idea' or 'Say it! Say
what you're thinking!' But then you think, 'I don't want to look stupid'
or, 'I don't want to sound like I know better than anyone else.'

Whether it's an idea, a suggestion, an observation or information that
could be helpful to other people, rather than look foolish, be challenged,
derided or ignored, you say nothing.

Sure, some people might not like what you have to say. So what? Do
you like what everyone else has to say? Probably not.

Share what you think or know. No one else may know. Just because no
one else has mentioned what you're thinking doesn't mean that it isn't
a good idea! If you don't speak up, if you wait for people to say something, the point may never get made at all and things might go in a
direction that you don't like or want.

It might also be the case that you're not alone in how you see things.
Others might share your ideas, insights and opinions, but also hesitate
to say something. But if you speak up, other people may agree and
support your idea, suggestion or observation.

In Practice

*Today I will behave as if this is the day I shall be
remembered. —Dr Seuss*

Build your confidence. Before you speak up with your opinions and
suggestions in meetings, look for opportunities to just ask a couple
of questions or for clarification about an issue. Work your way up to
sharing your opinions and ideas.

Prepare ahead of the meeting. Most meetings have a pre-set
agenda, so you know what will be discussed ahead of time. It doesn't
matter if you're not an expert on the subject of the meeting. Note
down and come prepared with a few thoughts and talking points. This
will help you feel more confident about your ideas and opinions
because you'll have had time to think beforehand.

Think of the questions and objections people might have and think
what your answers might be. Anticipating responses and questions will
give you the confidence to share the idea or opinion in the first place.

Take a deep breath and start to talk. Say in a clear, calm voice, 'I'd
like to say something.' The sooner you say what's on your mind, the
less time you have to talk yourself out of it. When you delay saying
anything, it can get harder to break into the discussion.

Know that not everyone will agree with what you have to say.
Don't let it discourage you from sharing your opinion in the future.
Even when you say something others don't agree with, you'll have
contributed to the discussion.

Get support. Before the meeting, ask a colleague to lend some
support when you speak up – maybe stopping someone interrupting
you by saying, 'Hang on, Jo. I'd like to hear what … has to say.'

SPEAKING OUT

Never be afraid to raise your voice for honesty and truth and compassion against injustice and lying and greed. If people all over the world ... would do this, it would change the earth. —William Faulkner

If speaking up is difficult – speaking out is more so!

Is there a difference between speaking up and speaking out? I think so. Speaking up is saying what you're thinking. It's expressing your ideas, observations and opinions. Speaking out is when you call someone to account or challenge a perceived wrongdoing either against yourself or someone else.

You may, for example, have concerns about something that's happening at work: unsafe procedures, corrupt practices, racism, bullying. It can be difficult to know what to do; challenging and whistleblowing come with risks and may lead you to think twice about speaking out. Thoughts such as, 'Is this really worth it?', 'What will I gain from this?', 'How will this hurt me in the long run?' run through your mind.

You may be opening a can of worms; exposing wrongdoing could create complications and more problems. You may create resentment, distance yourself from other people and be labelled a troublemaker. Sometimes it seems like staying silent is the wiser choice.

On the other hand, just one person speaking up can often be enough to encourage other dissenters to speak up too.

You may think that staying silent keeps you from being involved. But if the problem persists and you did nothing, you may then be the one called to account.

In Practice

Like a muddied spring or a polluted fountain is a righteous man who gives way before the wicked. —Proverbs 25:26

Draw on your values. Is the wrongdoing contrary to your values? If, for example, values such as fairness, equality, dignity, respect, inclusion, safety and kindness are important to you, then corruption and bullying are obviously not in line with – are the opposite of – what you intuitively know to be right. Do draw on your values to give you confidence to believe and know that by speaking out you *are* doing the right thing.

Have courage. If you see an unsafe practice or wrongdoing, can you challenge it there and then? If you feel you can speak out, do so. A firm, polite challenge is sometimes all that is needed. If, at work, you don't feel able to raise your concern with someone senior or no one is taking you seriously, consult your organisation's whistleblowing policy, if there is one, and follow that. (The term 'whistleblower' is used to describe people who make a 'qualifying disclosure' about a concern at work. See www.gov.uk/whistleblowing/who-to-tell-what-to-expect)

Get information and support. If it's a situation at work, you may want to get independent advice first, or contact your trade union or professional regulatory body. Go to Public Concern at Work (www.pcaw.co.uk).

If you're concerned about the safety of a child, contact the NSPCC (www.nspcc.org.uk) or Childline (www.childline.org.uk) for advice and a helpline number.

If you or someone you know is getting harassed in person or online, go to www.bullying.co.uk for advice and a helpline number.

If you have concerns about an older person, go to www.ageuk.org.uk/ for advice and a helpline number.

ASKING FOR WHAT YOU WANT

Be who you are and say what you feel, because those who mind don't matter and those who matter don't mind. —Dr Seuss

Do you want a particular birthday gift from a family member but feel impertinent asking for it? Maybe you want to ask for help with moving home? How about asking for time off work? Need an errand done? How can you get your colleague to do it during his lunch hour? Perhaps you want a friend to do the driving when you go out together at the weekend?

Are there situations where you'd like to feel more confident to assert yourself and ask for what you want? It isn't always easy to make requests; we worry that others will see us as needy, pushy or demanding, or that we'll be turned down and feel rejected and embarrassed as a result.

But you have a *right* to ask for what you want; to ask for what you like or need, to ask for what is proper or just. You have a right – you are *allowed* – to ask for what, to you, is appropriate or most convenient. Your feelings, likes, wants and needs are just as important as everyone else's and you have a right to express them.

If the builder, plumber or electrician you hired hasn't finished the work they agreed to do, you have a right to ask them to come back and complete the work. If you've lent something to a friend and they returned it to you damaged, you're allowed to ask them to fix it or replace it. You've reserved a table for dinner but you don't like where they've put you? You *are* allowed to ask to move.

If you wait for someone else to recognise what you need, you might wait forever. Sure, other people might turn you down; they have rights too! So what to do?

In many situations, thinking through in advance what you want and what you'll do if you don't get it will help give you the confidence to speak up.

In Practice

Stay strong. Stand Up. Have a voice. —Shawn Johnson

Before you say anything, think through the three things below. That way, you can sort out your thoughts to make sure that you don't miss anything.

Firstly, be clear what exactly it is that you want and why you want it. See if you can say it in just two or three sentences. Any more than that and you're probably going to be waffling. So, you might say, 'I need to take next Friday off. My Mum is very unwell and I need to visit her.'

Secondly, anticipate the other person's response. Decide how far you're prepared to negotiate and compromise if they're reluctant to cooperate. Decide what an alternative might be that works for you and benefits the other person as well. However, if you do choose to negotiate or compromise, bend as far as you can, but no further. Know what your limits are and stand your ground.

Thirdly, decide what you'll do if you don't get what you want. This is not about threats and punishments. Threats make an argument more likely. Instead, think about solutions. Ask yourself, 'What might be an alternative way forward?' 'What might be my plan B if I don't get what I've asked for?'

Build your confidence. Identify what you are only slightly uncomfortable asking for in a range of situations – at home, at work, in public and with service providers – and start with those situations.

SAYING NO

When you say 'yes' to others, make sure you're not saying 'no' to yourself. —Paulo Coelho

What's so hard about saying no to other people? Surely it's just a word, right? No. Often it's not that simple – not only can it hurt, anger or disappoint the other person, it can leave you feeling guilty – feeling you've done something wrong – when you say no to someone else's demand or request.

Maybe you find it difficult to let people down because you need their approval; you want people to like you so you do what you can to please them. It might be, for example, that you're often asked to work overtime but you're worried about letting down your colleagues and giving them extra work if you say no. Or your brother asks you to babysit. Again. He rarely asks anyone else but you don't want to say no and fall out with him. Perhaps a friend often asks you to give her lifts in your car and you feel that saying no would appear mean and selfish.

As a child, like most of us, you probably learnt that saying no was rude or selfish. 'Yes' was the polite and likeable thing to say. But you're an adult now; capable of making your own choices, as well as knowing the difference between wrong and right. Saying no doesn't mean you're a bad person; that you're being rude, mean, selfish or unkind. It's thinking like this which creates unhelpful beliefs that make it hard to say no.

But there are times you simply have to say 'no'. If you don't say 'no', or can't say 'no', you undermine your self-esteem and encourage others to take you for granted.

In Practice

Say no to everything, so you can say yes to the one thing. —Richie Norton

When someone asks you to do something, notice how you feel. Irritated? Worried? Anxious? Then you probably don't want to do it. Acknowledging how you feel about a particular situation can help you clarify what you do or don't want.

Ask for more time or information. If you're not sure how you feel, you may need to ask for more details about what the other person wants or you might need more time to think about it before you decide whether or not to say no.

If it's not an absolute 'yes', it's a 'no'. So say so. Use a firm, clear voice, make eye contact and simply say, 'No, I don't want to/can't do/ won't be able to ...' Don't waffle or give lots of excuses. You don't need to explain why you won't do something but if you do you only need one valid reason. Make your explanation honest and short.

Listen to the other person's response. Then, *you* respond in a way that will both acknowledge what they've said but also confirm you are standing firm. Say, for example, 'I know you need someone to babysit tomorrow (acknowledging) but I'm not able to do it' (standing firm).

Or, if you choose to, negotiate or compromise by saying what, if anything, you're prepared to do instead. For example, 'I'm not able to babysit. But I'd like to see the kids. Can you join us for lunch this Sunday?'

Practise. Think of three situations when you often want to say 'no'. Write out a brief 'no' response for each of those situations. Practise your response either by yourself or with a friend. You'll then feel more comfortable and ready to say 'no' the next time those situations arise.

LETTING SOMEONE DOWN

Bad news isn't wine. It doesn't improve with age. —Colin Powell

It's inevitable that throughout your life, at one time or another, whether you mean to or not, you're going to let people down and disappoint them – friends, family, colleagues or clients. It *is* going to happen.

Whether it's telling a client you can't meet the deadline, cancelling a night out with a friend or telling them that you've lost or broken something that belongs to them, whatever it is, giving someone bad news and letting them down is never a pleasant thing to have to do.

Often, it can be just as hard for you, the person giving the disappointing news, as it is for the person receiving it. How and when to tell them? How to manage their disappointment? What if they get upset and start crying? What if they're annoyed and start sulking or getting angry?

Sometimes, it's tempting to put off the bad news in the hope that things will change or improve. That way you can avoid telling them altogether. But holding back because you can't handle the other person's reaction or your embarrassment will only compound the problem.

As Lady Macbeth said to her husband – it's time to 'screw your courage to the sticking place.'

In Practice

Sometimes you have to let people down in order to get on.
Particularly in show business. —Dusty Springfield

Prepare what you're going to say. First, briefly explain what's led to to the situation. Setting the context – the circumstances relevant to the issue – can make a difference to how the bad news is grasped and understood. For example, 'I've got behind with my work.' Next, state the bad news simply and honestly, 'I'm sorry, I'm not going to be able to meet the deadline.'

Here's another example, again with the context and then the bad news. 'I decided to go for a swim. I forgot I was wearing the sunglasses you lent me. I'm afraid they fell off in the sea and I've lost them.'

Anticipate the reaction and questions the other person might have. 'How did you get behind with your work?' 'Have you been back to see if the sunglasses have been washed up onto the beach?'

Acknowledge their response. Acknowledge how the other person feels; 'I'm sorry you're upset. I can see this makes things difficult for you.' Do not, though, say, 'I know just how you feel,' or 'Try not to worry about it.' Although you might mean well, the other person may feel that actually you don't understand or that you're just trying to move off the subject.

Suggest what, if anything, you can do to help make up for letting them down. Think about this before you tell them the disappointing news. Maybe you could drop the price or do a piece of work for free for the client you're letting down? And your friend's lost sunglasses – surely you're going to offer to buy them a new pair?

DEALING WITH CRITICISM

There is only one way to avoid criticism. Do nothing, say nothing and be nothing. —Aristotle

We all get hit by other people's slings and arrows from time to time. They can come from any direction – a family member, friend, colleague or a complete stranger. Maybe it's someone who is always firing off and always finds something wrong. Perhaps, though, it seems to come from nowhere and catches you by surprise.

How do you respond when someone aims a criticism at you? Do you return the attack? Do you vehemently defend yourself? Or do you shrink and crumble?

Of course, your response to criticism often depends on who it is that's criticising you, what they're criticising you for and why, when and where they're being critical. But whatever and whenever it is, it's not nice to be told you're not doing, looking, saying or behaving as someone else thinks you should. Criticism can really knock your confidence and self-esteem, particularly if it's unfair.

On the one hand, you can see criticism as someone else's problem; their problem is that they don't like or approve of something you've done or said. On the other hand, criticism is a kind of feedback; an evaluation; the other person's genuine experience and perspective of you; what you've done or said. OK, it might not all be accurate and the other person may be harsh and may have exaggerated, but there still may be seeds of truth in their criticism.

Rather than let it knock your confidence and self-esteem, you can learn a more positive way to handle criticism.

In Practice

Let me never fall into the vulgar mistake of dreaming that I am persecuted whenever I am contradicted. —Ralph Waldo Emerson

Next time someone criticises you, listen carefully. Imagine that someone said, 'Whenever you're talking with other people, you never ask anyone about themselves. It's always about you. You're self-centred and boring.'

Clarify. Before you respond to the accusation, if you're not clear what exactly the other person is criticising you about, ask them, 'I just need to be clear; do you think I'm not interested in other people?' This gives the other person the chance to agree: 'Yes. In fact I think you're a narcissist.' (!) Or they can clarify what they mean: 'I think you *are* interested. But only if they've got something to offer you.'

Be honest, could any of it be true? Instead of reacting immediately by defending yourself or going on the attack, stop. Stop for a second and ask yourself: Could there be any truth in the accusation?

Ask how they want the problem solved. If they haven't said so already, ask the other person what they suggest you do to put things right. You might agree with their solution or you might not.

Respond. Say whatever you think is valid in the criticism. Say if you agree with their solution or suggest your own. For example, you might respond to the narcissist criticism with, 'I'm not a narcissist. You're right though, I don't often ask people about their lives. I'm going to make an effort to do so at the party tomorrow.'

If you honestly feel that their criticism is unfair and invalid, say so. Calmly tell the other person you understand that's their perspective and how or why their criticism is unfair or wrong. Or say nothing and let it go. Most likely their mind is already made up and nothing you say will change it.

GIVING CONSTRUCTIVE CRITICISM

You have to lift a person up before you can really put them in their place. —Criss Jami

Have you ever been asked your opinion on something, but didn't say anything or even lied because you felt sure that if you said what you really thought, it would end in an argument?

Maybe someone asked you what you thought about what they were wearing, something they'd created, a performance they'd given or a piece of work they'd completed. They said they really wanted your honest opinion but you didn't know how to say it in a way that would avoid one or both of you getting hurt, angry or resentful.

Nobody likes being told that they're doing things the wrong way, but if the other person has failed to meet a particular standard, or has done it wrong or incorrectly or it's just not to your taste, how can you turn a potentially difficult, awkward situation into something more positive? How, exactly, do you give constructive criticism? By thinking differently about what criticism is.

Most of us think of criticism as a negative, unfavourable judgement. It's not nice. But if you reframe the concept of criticism – think of it more positively – you start off on a better foot. Rather than think in terms of what someone's done wrong, think in terms of what they can do right; what changes they could make that would make things even better.

In Practice

People seldom refuse help if one offers it in the right way. —A. C. Benson

Firstly, decide what, exactly, the problem is and secondly, decide what the solution is. Consider, for example, this criticism: 'Your presentation went on and on. You kept repeating yourself. You're going to need to do some work on it before you give that talk again.'

This is not constructive criticism! Constructive criticism describes what, specifically, can be changed in order to improve and make things better. A more positive way to say it would be, 'I thought you made some good points but they could be more brief. You went over time by about 10 minutes. Perhaps time it to five minutes per point, and then have five minutes left for closing. This would create a presentation that's more balanced.'

Use the word 'and.' Start with something positive then add the word 'and' to make your suggestion for improvement. Look at these remarks: 'I love the design, layout, and intro video on the new website. *But* the sidebar content needs to be less cluttered; you need to narrow it down to the key things. Also the font size should be increased.'

'But' is a minimising word that detracts from the positive sentence before it. In this example, the word 'but' has taken away from the fact that so much about the website was good. Replacing the word 'but' with 'and' creates a much more positive meaning. 'And' is positive and infers there's a helpful suggestion to come. 'I love the design, layout, and intro video on the new website *and* if the sidebar content was narrowed down to the key points and the font size increased it would be great!'

Replacing the word 'but' with 'and' is a neat little trick because the word 'and' forces you to complete the sentence in a positive way.

PREPARING FOR
A JOB INTERVIEW

Whenever you are asked if you can do a job, tell 'em, 'Certainly I can!'
Then get busy and find out how to do it. —Theodore Roosevelt

If the mere thought of being interviewed for a job or a course makes you feel weak and wobbly, you're not alone. Most people dread job interviews; they get themselves worked up, worried and anxious, telling themselves things like, '*I'll talk too quickly,*' '*I'll dry up,*' '*I won't know the answers to the questions,*' '*They won't like me, other applicants are going to be so much better than me,*' '*I don't have everything they're asking for.*'

Would you say the same things to a friend who was going to an interview? Why not? Because you know it would seriously knock their confidence and self-esteem and their ability to do well in the interview. So why do it to yourself?

After all, they called you; they decided your application form or your CV and cover letter were worthy of an interview. You wouldn't have been invited to interview if they didn't seriously think you capable or good enough. Remind yourself of this.

Change your beliefs and expectations and be kinder to yourself. Instead of seeing the interview as an interrogation, think of it as a conversation; a conversation with questions and answers and an exchange of information about a job.

In Practice

'During job interviews, when they ask: "What is your worst quality?" I always say: "Flatulence". That way I get my own office.' —Dan Thompson

Be prepared. Read the company's website and social media feeds. Learn about the company's products, markets, culture and competitors. Familiarising yourself of this will not only show you've done your homework but also help you devise your own questions.

Read your application form again. You need to remember what you've written and think about what questions might come from that. Imagine some of the interview questions and rehearse possible answers to questions, such as, 'Why do you want this job?' 'What skills and strengths will you bring to this job?' 'What do you think the challenges of this job would be and how would you cope?'

Use confident body language. Become SuperYou. Practise a 'power pose'. Just before the interview, go to the loo and strike an heroic pose for two minutes. Stand with your feet apart, place your hands on your hips, back straight, chest out and head up like you're Superman or Wonder Woman. Stand like this for one or two minutes. You'll be amazed at how the powerful posture can help your confidence. Try it right now. It's a very effective technique.

Practise shaking hands with a friend. A limp hand shake signals low confidence and self-esteem. You'll need to shake hands firmly, look the interviewer in the eyes and clearly say, 'Hello'.

Listen to music. If you want to come across as calm and thoughtful, listen to calm music on your way to the interview. If you want to come across as energetic and enthusiastic, listen to upbeat music.

Dress for how you want to feel. Don't dress in clothes you feel awkward wearing; you'll just come across as awkward.

Get support. Before your interview, ask a friend to give you a pep talk to help you feel good about yourself. It can really help!

SPEAKING IN PUBLIC

According to most studies, people's number one fear is public speaking. Number two is death. Death is number two. Does that sound right? This means, to the average person, if you go to a funeral, you're better off in the casket than doing the eulogy. —Jerry Seinfeld

Whether it's giving a speech at a social or professional occasion, there are few things people dislike more than public speaking. Thoughts, such as, 'Something will go wrong, I'll forget my words. I'll talk too quickly and I'm going to sound nervous. People will see I'm nervous. They'll think I'm weird and pathetic' create anxiety that can undermine your confidence.

Why are so many of us so scared of public speaking? We're afraid of doing it all wrong and being humiliated. We're aware that if we make a mistake, go blank, stutter or simply bore people to tears, there are 10, 20 or maybe a hundred pairs of eyes on us. That's dozens of times more humiliation than we would ever face when talking to just one other person!

All eyes are on you. You have to give a monologue – literally – you have to speak alone. And that's not natural, is it? What feels more natural is a dialogue – a conversation where you take it in turns to speak – exchange experiences, ideas and opinions with another person.

Talking to just one or two people, you can tell you if they don't understand or like what you're saying, you can explain and clarify, ask and answer questions. But when you're speaking to a group, you can't really tell how each and every person is receiving you – some may like what you have to say but others may not. And if they don't, what can you do about it? Not a lot.

How can you increase your confidence around public speaking? The usual, good advice is to prepare and practise. But another important approach is to let go of needing other people's approval.

In Practice

You can please some of the people all of the time, you can please all of the people some of the time, but you can't please all of the people all of the time. —John Lydgate

Simplify. Most speakers try to do too much in a speech. That then gives them far too much to think about – they worry about leaving something out or losing their train of thought. Don't try and cram too much in. Aim, instead, to keep it short and simple. Firstly, write down, in one sentence, what your talk is about. Secondly, what the main points you want to make are. However long you have – 10 minutes or an hour – plan to get three or four points across. If you have an hour, spend up to 15 minutes on each point. If you have 10 minutes, spend 2 minutes on each point.

Write out notes to refer to during your talk – use bullet points and key words as prompts to remind you of the next point, and then elaborate.

Rehearse your presentation – to yourself at first and then in front of a friend or colleague. Ask for honest feedback; what's good and what can be improved?

Expect to be nervous. Even experienced speakers get nervous. Imagine you're explaining your main ideas to a friend – the friend who helped you rehearse. Don't rush. Try to speak fairly slowly and remember to pause after each key point. Listen to Barack Obama; he does this very effectively.

Focus on nice people. Look out at the audience and find a few people who are nodding along with your story or points. There's a real sense of reassurance when someone is agreeing with you. Although your audience may be a hundred people, focus on one friendly face at a time; for a few seconds at a time.

HELPING OTHER PEOPLE

We are all here on earth to help others; what on earth the others are here for I don't know. —W. H. Auden

Think of a time you helped out another person. What did you do? Maybe you helped someone with some work they were struggling with. Perhaps you explained something to someone and made a difficult concept easier to understand. Were you able to help someone in need, someone in pain or distress? Perhaps you simply did someone a favour. Whatever it was, after you'd helped them, how did you feel?

Helping someone else – whether it's holding a door open for someone or helping them through a serious difficulty – can make you and the person you are helping feel good.

Helping others – a colleague, a family member, a friend or even a stranger – improves how you see yourself; you see yourself making a positive contribution and doing good. When you help support other people, you can feel uplifted and valued.

Often, your kind remarks, good deed or contribution will be acknowledged and appreciated by the person you've helped. But even if you're not directly thanked or shown appreciation for your kindness and consideration, you can still feel good about yourself and what you were able to do because *you* know that you supported someone and made a positive difference.

The aim is not to impress or seek approval. It's not about being subservient either – that just invites people to use you, which only serves to erode your self-esteem. It's simply about making a positive contribution and experiencing the good feelings that come with connecting with – and helping – other people.

In Practice

No one is useless in this world who lightens the burdens of another. —Charles Dickens

Anticipate what others might need. Helping others can range from giving someone encouragement or advice to giving practical help. It might just be a small kindness; if, for example, a colleague was bogged down with work that day, you could simply fetch him a coffee. Perhaps a friend has been going through a difficult time – invite them out for a drink or a meal, a film, a show or a walk in the country. Help a neighbour in need by picking up some shopping once a week, or offer to cut their grass. Don't feel you have to rescue the other person or make their situation your own, just make a thoughtful gesture of kindness and consideration.

Ask if you can help. People often find it difficult to ask for help. They feel that they're inconveniencing the other person or being a burden. Simply ask how you could help make a situation better. If you have already thought of something you could do that might help, it might be appropriate to ask first if they are OK with you helping out in that way.

Volunteer. There's a huge range of volunteer opportunities available. Whether it's helping at a local community food project or an animal rescue centre, supporting adults to learn to read or children to practise for their cycling proficiency test, volunteering connects you with local people and activities.

Find out about volunteering opportunities near to you by visiting your local volunteer centre or going to https://do-it.org/. For many would-be helpers, the most difficult thing is getting started. So ask a friend or family member to sign up with you as a fellow helper.

ASKING FOR HELP

The only mistake you can make is not asking for help. —Sandeep Jauhar

Do you ask for help when you don't know how to do something or can't manage it on your own? Or, rather than look stupid and incompetent, do you pretend like you know what you're doing? Perhaps you think asking for help is a sign of weakness; that if you ask for help you're admitting you're inadequate in some way; that you lack knowledge, skill or experience to do something yourself. You don't want anyone to see that you're struggling; you want people to think that you're in control and can handle things.

You get in your own way if you make asking for help mean something negative about you when it doesn't. Asking for help doesn't mean you're stupid or inadequate, it simply means you need help with something specific for a time.

Instead of seeing that we are giving others an opportunity to contribute, we think that asking for help means we are a burden.

But confident people often ask others for help, not only because they're secure enough to let it be known they need help but they know that trying to do everything themselves is not always the best use of their time, skills or energy and that it can leave them feeling overwhelmed and stressed and then they can't do things properly. Confident people find someone who's good at what they need to learn or get done and then ask for their help and guidance. They know that asking, 'Can you help me?' shows respect for the other person's knowledge and abilities. Otherwise, they wouldn't ask.

Refusing to ask for help is counter-productive; you're more likely to berate yourself when you can't get it done well or on time, which only serves to knock your self-esteem and confidence further.

In Practice

Refusing to ask for help when you need it is refusing someone the chance to be helpful. —Rick Okasek

Change your beliefs and expectations. Telling yourself, 'I should know and be able to do this. They're going to think I'm hopeless if I ask for help' is unrealistic. More empowering beliefs that will encourage you to ask for help are, 'Of course I don't know everything. Asking for help is responsible, to me and to others. I can get things done well if I ask someone else to help me.'

Tell yourself that asking for help is less embarrassing than failing at whatever you're finding difficult.

If the problem you're seeking help for is an aspect of a team project or social event, know that you're letting other people down by not seeking help; you're not the only one affected if you refuse to seek help.

Make it easy for someone to help you. Ask the right person for their help – someone who has the ability, knowledge or time. (Don't ask someone who'll make you feel stupid for asking.)

Be direct – don't drop hints, sigh or look sad. Clearly explain what you need help with. Don't waffle or apologise for needing help. Don't say, 'I know you're really busy, so only if you have time ... only if you want to ... sorry, I know this is a lot to ask ...' Talking like this infers that you don't consider yourself, your time or the request to be valuable. Instead, simply say, 'I need help with ... would you be able to ... by tomorrow for me?' This way, the person is clear about what, how and when to help you.

Practise asking for help. Make a list of what you could ask for help with: the laundry? Walking the dog? Maybe you need help to manage a health condition? Ask for help!

DEALING WITH BULLIES

When they go low you go high. —Michelle Obama

If someone is persistently badgering, dominating or intimidating you, someone is continually coercing and threatening you, criticising or humiliating you or making abusive remarks and insulting you, you're being bullied. Whether it's happening to you in person or online, being the victim of a bully can be a devastating experience.

Whatever their reason for doing it, all bullies have one thing in common: they create fear and misery. And the longer they bully you, the more your confidence and self-esteem is affected and prevents you from doing something. And you *must* do something. This person will not go away!

If you are a victim of bullying, their behaviour is entirely their responsibility, not yours, no matter what the bully may tell you. But, you *do* have a responsibility; your responsibility is to protect yourself from the mental, emotional and social harm that the bully is causing you.

It's a waste of time trying to change a bully, or understand how they came to enjoy such cruel behaviour. To stop the bullying you must choose not to be a victim. It's a fight or flight situation.

In Practice

When people hurt you over and over, think of them like sand paper.
They may scratch and hurt you a bit, but in the end, you end up
polished and they end up useless. —Chris Colfer

Fight. Some battles just can't be fought alone. Staying silent and telling no one will only isolate you while at the same time empowering the bully, so you must get help and support. Don't be afraid to do this. There are people who can give you support and advice. There are organisations that specialise in supporting anyone who is being bullied or abused. There's a list of websites for support and information in cases of bullying and abuse at the back of this book.

Take flight. Think seriously about leaving; leaving the job, the neighbourhood, the relationship or the social media account. By walking away, you put yourself in a positive position; one of being in control. You take away the opportunity for the bully to continue their behaviour.

Identify your values and goals. Decide what's most important to you – beating the bully or keeping yourself safe and sane? Think about the good things that can happen if you choose to leave the situation. Yes, you might have to walk away from a good job, financial stability, friends etc. but focus on the positive; that you've left the bully behind. Once you've left them you can put your energy into finding a new job or somewhere to live instead of spending your energy trying to please, pacify or avoid the bully.

Minimise the chances of being bullied in future. Learn how to be assertive. There may be an assertiveness course near you. There are also books (I've written two: *How to be Assertive* and *Dealing with Difficult People*) that can help you maintain your boundaries and avoid being bullied in future.

GETTING RESPECT

Respect is earned. Honesty is appreciated. Trust is gained. Loyalty is returned. —Author unknown

Respect. You want it, you need it and you deserve it. We all want to be respected but how do we get it? How do we earn it? And what exactly *is* 'respect'?

Respect happens when one person has regard and consideration for another. If someone respects you, they think you have worth and value; they think you matter. They demonstrate their respect – or lack of it – by *what* they say to you and the *way* they speak to you. Their *attitude* towards you and how they respond and behave towards you tells you whether they think that your needs and wishes, beliefs and opinions, abilities and contributions have worth and value.

You get respect from others as a result of the things you do and don't do and the way you behave towards others.

Earning respect involves taking responsibility for your own behaviour and responses. It involves having boundaries and limits for how you allow other people to treat you. It's not easy if you have low self-esteem, but you've got to start somewhere.

In Practice

You teach people how to treat you by what you allow, what you stop and what you reinforce. —Tony Gaskins

Think about the people you respect. What is it about them – what personal qualities and abilities do they have, do you admire and think are worthy? While your values might differ in some ways from theirs, be inspired by what you admire in others.

Identify your values and live by them. What do you believe in? What's important to you in the way you live your life and behave towards others? Earn respect by behaving with integrity. This means being honest, reliable and dependable, honouring your commitments and promises; walking the walk, not just talking the talk. Whether it's speaking up and speaking out; standing up for others; being kind, courageous and compassionate; accepting differences of opinion or showing appreciation, there are countless ways you can show and earn the respect of others.

Treat others with respect even if they won't do the same for you. Listen to them, take their needs and wishes into consideration. When you treat others with respect, most of them will appreciate the consideration you show and may respond in kind. And those that don't treat you with respect? Keep your distance, but when you do have to interact with them, treat them with respect. Others will see it and respect you for it.

Have boundaries and limits. Be considerate of other people's needs and situations but set limits and boundaries. Have self-respect; when you say no, you show that you value and respect your needs, time and commitments. What are you willing and unwilling to accept in terms of other people's needs, demands and behaviour? In a variety of situations, you need to know how far is too far. It doesn't mean that you should cut yourself off, but if you don't know what your limits are, how can you know if you're being flexible or just being a doormat?

MAKING NEW FRIENDS

*Remember that every good friend was once a
stranger. —Author unknown*

Most of us make use of some form of social media, giving us a constant opportunity to share details of our lives with dozens, if not hundreds of 'friends.' But friends that are solely virtual aren't the same as friendships in the real world.

Real friendships are important for our well-being. Humans are inherently social creatures; we're wired to benefit from close relationships – to make attachments – with other people: family, partners and, of course, friends.

Friends can be many things; people have different ideas of what friendship means. But generally a friend is a person with whom you have a bond of mutual affection, regard and support. You also share experiences and one or more outside interests. Not only do you share interests but you're also interested in each other; you care about what's happened and is happening in a friend's life.

If you're low on confidence and self-esteem, making new friends isn't always easy. It takes effort on your part; you need to be willing to meet others, to be yourself and give something of yourself. You *can* make new friends but you can't sit and wait for other people to come to you. You need to get out there!

In Practice

I get by with a little help from my friends. —John Lennon

Start with your interests. When you have interests and activities you enjoy, you can meet people with similar interests. Whether it's tennis or Japanese cooking, it makes it easier for you to talk to others and make friends because you share similar interests and values.

Go to www.meetup.com which will enable you to find and join groups of people in your local area who share your interests. There are groups to fit a wide range of interests and hobbies, plus others you'll never have thought of. There are book groups, art groups, film groups, sci fi groups, gardening groups, singing groups and cycling groups.

People who go to 'meet-ups' do so knowing they'll be meeting others who are also open to making new friends. If you find people who are just as keen on, for example, board games, hiking or craft beers as you are, then you'll find it relatively easy to connect and make friends with them. And when you're doing something that's fun and meaningful, your ability to form connections will feel natural.

Get support. Ask a friend or colleague to come with you to an event or meet-up. Having a familiar face can help you to feel more confident. Just don't stay with them the whole time, otherwise you'll never talk to anyone else!

Volunteer. Volunteering is also a good way to meet people and make friends. By working together you meet and create bonds with people who want to make a contribution to the lives of others, so you have a common cause.

Reach out. As you meet and make friends, take the initiative and, at some point, invite a couple of people out or over to your house for curry or pizza, to the pub or to an event related to your shared interests.

ABOUT THE AUTHOR

Gill Hasson is a teacher, trainer and writer. She has 20 years' experience in the area of personal development. Her expertise is in the areas of confidence and self-esteem, communication skills, assertiveness and resilience.

Gill delivers teaching and training for educational organisations, voluntary and business organisations and the public sector.

Gill is the author of the bestselling *Mindfulness* and *Emotional Intelligence* plus other books on the subjects of dealing with difficult people, resilience, communication skills and assertiveness.

Gill's particular interest and motivation is in helping people to realise their potential, to live their best life! You can contact Gill via her website www.gillhasson.co.uk or email her at gillhasson@btinternet.com.

MORE QUOTES

Why fit in when you were born to stand out? —Dr Seuss

All you need in this life is ignorance and confidence, and then success is sure. —Mark Twain

Low self-confidence isn't a life sentence. Self-confidence can be learned, practiced, and mastered – just like any other skill. Once you master it, everything in your life will change for the better. —Barrie Davenport

No matter how many mistakes you make or how slow you progress, you're still way ahead of anyone who isn't trying. —Tony Robbins

Trust yourself. Create the kind of self that you will be happy to live with all your life. Make the most of yourself by fanning the tiny, inner sparks of possibility into flames of achievement. —Golda Meir

You are what you think and what you think, you are. —Author unknown

Nobody can go back and start a new beginning, but anyone can start today and make a new ending. —Maria Robinson

People are like stained-glass windows. They sparkle and shine when the sun is out, but when the darkness sets in their true beauty is revealed only if there is light from within. —Elisabeth Kubler-Ross

To anyone that ever told you you're no good. They're no better. —Hayley Williams

Nobody can make you feel inferior without your consent. —Eleanor Roosevelt

Your time is limited, so don't waste it living someone else's life. —Steve Jobs

To be yourself in a world that is constantly trying to make you something else is the greatest accomplishment. —Ralph Waldo Emerson

You wouldn't worry so much about what others think of you if you realized how seldom they do. —Eleanor Roosevelt

So many people along the way, whatever it is you aspire to do, will tell you it can't be done. But all it takes is imagination. You dream. You plan. You reach. —Michael Phelps

I want to be around people that do things. I don't want to be around people anymore that judge or talk about what people do. I want to be around people that dream and support and do things. —Amy Poehler

When I was growing up I always wanted to be someone. Now I realize I should have been more specific. —Lily Tomlin

Doubt kills more dreams than failure ever will. —Suzy Kassem

One important key to success is self-confidence. An important key to self-confidence is preparation. —Arthur Ashe

If we all did the things we are capable of doing, we would literally astound ourselves. —Thomas Alva Edison

Shyness has a strange element of narcissism, a belief that how we look, how we perform, is truly important to other people. —Andre Dubus

Trust yourself. You know more than you think you do. —Dr Benjamin Spock

Successful people have fear, successful people have doubts, and successful people have worries. They just don't let these feelings stop them. —T. Harv Eker

You can have anything you want if you are willing to give up the belief that you can't have it. —Dr Robert Anthony

It is not the mountain we conquer, but ourselves. —Sir Edmund Hillary

Inaction breeds doubt and fear. Action breeds confidence and courage. If you want to conquer fear, do not sit home and think about it. Go out and get busy. —Dale Carnegie

Confidence is a habit that can be developed by acting as if you already had the confidence you desire to have. —Brian Tracy

Twenty years from now you will be more disappointed by the things you didn't do than by the ones you did do. So throw off the bowlines. Sail away from the safe harbor. Catch the trade winds in your sail. Explore. Dream. Discover. —Mark Twain

If things in your life don't add up, start subtracting. —Anon

It is one of the most beautiful compensations of this life that no man can seriously help another without helping himself. —Charles Dudley Warner

If you live for people's acceptance you'll die from their rejection. —Lecrae

You have no responsibility to live up to what other people think you ought to accomplish. I have no responsibility to be like they expect me to be. It's their mistake, not my failing. —Richard P. Feynman

Care about what other people think and you will always be their prisoner. —Lao Tzu

People are like dirt. They can either nourish you and help you grow as a person, or they can stunt your growth and make you wilt and die. —Plato

It ain't what they call you, it's what you answer to. —W.C. Fields

What lies behind us and what lies before us are tiny matters compared to what lies within us. —Ralph Waldo Emerson

You're always with yourself, so you might as well enjoy the company. —Diane Von Furstenberg

The better you feel about yourself, the less you feel the need to show off. —Robert Hand

Because one believes in oneself, one doesn't try to convince others. Because one is content with oneself, one doesn't need others' approval. Because one accepts oneself, the whole world accepts him or her. —Wayne Dyer

Most of the shadows of this life are caused by standing in one's own sunshine. —Ralph Waldo Emerson

When I loved myself enough, I began leaving whatever wasn't healthy. This meant people, jobs, my own beliefs and habits - anything that kept me small. My judgement called it disloyal. Now I see it as self-loving. —Kim McMillen

One's destination is never a place, but a new way of seeing things. —Henry Miller

Slow down. Haste is a form of violence toward the self. —Author unknown

This is your world. Shape it, or someone else will. —Gary Lew

Be brave. Take risks. Nothing can substitute experience. —Paulo Coelho

The biggest risk is not taking any risk ... In a world that's changing really quickly, the only strategy that is guaranteed to fail is not taking risks. —Mark Zuckerberg

Believe in yourself and there will come a day when others will have no choice but to believe with you. —Cynthia Kersey

Courage is not the absence of fear, but rather the judgement that something else is more important than fear. —Ambrose Redmoon

Confidence comes not from always being right but from not fearing to be wrong. —Peter T. McIntyre

The way to develop self-confidence is to do the thing you fear and get a record of successful experiences behind you. —William Jennings Bryan

If you hear a voice within you say 'you cannot paint,' then by all means paint, and that voice will be silenced. —Vincent Van Gogh

Whether you think that you can, or that you can't, you are usually right. —Henry Ford

Push your limits ... it reminds ourselves that we are living. —Michele Valentine

Sometimes the hardest part isn't letting go but rather learning to start over. —Nicole Sobon

There's an important difference between giving up and letting go. —Jessica Hatchigan

Being comfortable isn't the way to learn to expand your abilities. —Thomas Perry

A ship is always safe at the shore – but that is not what it is built for. —Albert Einstein

Treat all of life like a near-death experience. That's what it is. —Donald Miller

If you want something new you have to stop doing something old. —Peter F. Druckner

Some people say you are going the wrong way, when it's simply a way of your own. —Angelina Jolie

When it comes down to it, I let them think what they want. If they care enough to bother with what I do, then I'm already better than them. —Marilyn Monroe

Courage is the power to let go of the familiar. —Raymond Lindquist

What would happen if you gave yourself permission to do something you've never done before? There's only one way to find out. —Gina Greenlee

I can't change the direction of the wind, but I can adjust my sails to always reach my destination. —James Dean

Never give in, never give in, never, never, never, never – in nothing, great or small, large or petty, never give in except to convictions of honour and good sense. —Winston Churchill

The people that quit when they get knocked down from life's blows call it failure. The people that get up and keep on moving forward towards their goals and desires call it experience. —Mike Kemski

Our deepest fear is not that we are inadequate. Our deepest fear is that we are powerful beyond measure. It is our light, not our darkness that most frightens us. We ask ourselves, Who am I to be brilliant, gorgeous, talented, and fabulous? Actually, who are you not to be? You are a child of God. Your playing small does not serve the world. There is nothing enlightened about shrinking so that other people will not feel insecure around you. We are all meant to shine, as children do. We were born to make manifest the glory of God that is within us. It is not just in some of us; it is in everyone and as we let our own light shine, we unconsciously give others permission to do the same. As we are liberated from our own fear, our presence automatically liberates others. —Marianne Williamson

USEFUL WEBSITES

If you are being bullied:

> www.bullying.co.uk/
> https://www.gov.uk/workplace-bullying-and-harassment

If you're a child or young person being bullied:

> www.nspcc.org.uk
> www.childline.org.uk

If you're worried about an older person being bullied or abused:

> www.gov.uk/report-abuse-of-older-person
> https://elderabuse.org.uk/

If you are experiencing domestic abuse:

> www.womensaid.org.uk

If you'd like advice about reporting unsafe practices or corruption at work:

> www.gov.uk/whistleblowing/who-to-tell-what-to-expect
> www.pcaw.co.uk

If you'd like information about careers and studying

> nationalcareersservice.direct.gov.uk
> www.hotcourses.com/

If you'd like to do voluntary work:

> https://do-it.org/